A Maniac Commodity Trader's Guide to Making a Fortune

A Not-So-Crazy Road Map to Riches

KEVIN KERR

BICENTENNIAL
1807
WILEY
2007
BICENTENNIAL

John Wiley & Sons, Inc.

Published by John Wiley & Sons, Inc., Hoboken, New Jersey
Published simultaneously in Canada

For general information on our other products and services or for technical support, please contact our Customer Care Department within the United States at (800) 762-2974, outside the United States at (317) 572-3993 or fax (317) 572-4002.

Wiley also publishes its books in a variety of electronic formats. Some content that appears in print may not be available in electronic books. For more information about Wiley products, visit our web site at www.wiley.com.

Library of Congress Cataloging-in-Publication Data:

Kerr, Kevin.
  A maniac commodity trader's guide to making a fortune : a not-so crazy roadmap to riches / Kevin Kerr.
    p. cm.
  ISBN 978-0-471-77190-6 (cloth)
   1. Commodity exchanges. I. Title.
  HG6046.K45 2007
  332.64'4—dc22   2006036643

Printed in the United States of America

10 9 8 7 6 5 4 3 2 1

I would like to dedicate this book to my good friends the Butler brothers, David, Thomas, and Timothy, who have always treated me as family and who introduced me to the amazing world of commodities on the New York Cotton Exchange all those years ago. I am eternally grateful.

CONTENTS

CHAPTER 1

―――――

COMMODITY MARKETS

YOU CAN'T AFFORD TO IGNORE THEM ANYMORE

The commodity market mystique is alive and well. Stellar successes and dismal failures in these markets are the stuff of legends. From an outsider's perspective, commodity markets can be intimidating, even scary. I'm here to dispel some of the common myths and misconceptions about these markets. I can with all authority tell you that these markets are some of the most liquid, well-ordered, and secure in the world today. And once you've read this book, you'll agree that adding commodities to your portfolio is a sure way to capitalize on some of the most rewarding, exciting investment opportunities ever. Even if you don't know preferred stock from livestock, this book will introduce you to an asset class that promises to be a vital part of your portfolio over the next 20 years, and beyond.

Some people call me the Maniac Trader. I'm flattered. Why? Well, to most people these fast-paced markets conjure up images of high-risk investing in an environment of absolute chaos. Actually, the images of chaos and high risk are two myths I will dispel in this book. I trade all commodities and I trade both sides of the market, switching from the bear camp to the bull camp and then back again, sometimes within only a few days. Some would call this a schizophrenic existence. But it definitely works for me, and it can work for you if you take the time to learn about and trade these highly liquid, exceedingly profitable markets. Read on . . .

A LITTLE HISTORY

Commodity markets in various forms have been around forever, or at least since the time of ancient Greece and Rome. They even survived the Dark Ages, and reemerged at local fairs in medieval times, arranged by trade associations formed by merchants, craftsmen, and promoters. Over the next few centuries, these markets evolved into exchanges, or *bourses,* in England and Europe, as well as in Japan and the New World. U.S. cash commodity exchanges first appeared in New York for trading in domestic produce.

Though none of these markets exist now, they were the foundation for the commodity markets as we know them today. Since 1848, when the Chicago Board of Trade was formed, commodity futures have given producers and consumers a way to even out price moves and protect against market risk, as well as giving investors a way to capitalize on market moves.

In their early days, futures markets were used primarily to make or take delivery of the actual commodity; today, fewer than 1 percent of all futures contracts actually result in delivery against the contract. So there's really no truth to the myth that you'll end up with 200 head of hungry cattle grazing on your front lawn, or 50,000 gallons of orange juice cooling in your fridge, or a boxcar of grain dumped in your backyard! Unless, of course, that's what you want.

RESOURCES, NATURALLY

Right now, the world is experiencing a commodities supercycle— a boom in resources that's likely to last for at least another decade. The market for raw resources is raging—because of China, because of

India, because of surging oil demand and plunging energy supplies and the crushing effect of hurricanes on offshore U.S. oil. It's time for you to get in on the profit cycle!

History is full of gear-turning, gut-churning events, each with its own importance. But each is connected to the others by an endless cycle of supply and demand. As the world scrambles for resources, the opportunities for the savvy investor to profit are endless. And because these products are finite, we can expect demand to continue to grow. At this moment, you're looking at one of the best times in history to make money by trading resources.

Let's face it—trading commodities is not for the meek or faint of heart. You need sound judgment, guts, and an appetite for risk, not to mention available capital. These markets move, and they move quickly. Just take a look at all the markets over the past few months—gold, oil, grains, stock indexes, tropical markets, all of them with wild swings in both directions. There are huge risks but incredible rewards for the savvy trader or investor.

Cycles in commodities can be very predictable. There are no CEOs on the inside cooking the books. There are no accounting firms puffing up profit reports. You just have the commodities on the move. Trading on those moves, you can make money no matter which way prices are headed.

Many times in this book I refer to commodities trading as "the last bastion of pure capitalism on earth." I mean, where else can you sell something you don't own, buy it back half an hour later, and walk away with 100 percent profit? Few investment vehicles offer the excitement, flexibility, and tremendous profit opportunities of commodities.

STORM OF PROFITS

It's unfortunate, but profit opportunities often are greatest when things go wrong. Look at the devastation from Hurricane Katrina. When hurricane season is in full swing it can be a very long summer indeed. Often, Gulf Coast residents have barely picked up the pieces from the previous year's debacle when it is time to batten down the hatches yet again.

In 2005, four Category 3 storms—Dennis, Katrina, Rita, and Wilma—left a trail of havoc and destruction through a large part of the United States. Hurricane Katrina's strong winds and heavy waves devastated the Gulf Coast in late August. The storm and resulting flooding caused more than 1,300 deaths and an estimated $100 billion in damage, making it the most expensive natural disaster in U.S. history.

Nobody can predict for sure what any storm season will hold, but some experts say we are in the beginning stages of a hurricane supercycle, which usually lasts 15 to 20 years.

Stockpiling positions in some of the key commodities that may be adversely affected can be a very profitable strategy. As certain industries brace for each new storm season, traders can hedge themselves by adding specific commodities to their portfolios on a limited basis, using options or even futures to some extent.

Don't feel guilty betting on a rough hurricane season; after all, like any type of hedging, it's insurance. When we purchase fire insurance on our houses, we don't hope they'll burn down, at least not usually. No, we take out insurance to protect our investment—that's all we're doing.

The vulnerable markets include everything from natural gas and sugar to orange juice and crude oil. Take sugar, for example. Sugar crops have sustained hard hits in Florida and elsewhere from recent years' hurricanes. Sugar has the added benefit of being a key ingredient in the production of ethanol and is already in high demand, so there's a double whammy here. Another market likely to be heavily impacted by a rough hurricane season is natural gas. Remember, natural gas is used for heating and cooling—again, a double-edged sword.

Another good risk/reward scenario heading into an active hurricane season would be adding some unleaded gasoline call options to your portfolio. Whoa! I know what you may be saying: "Oh, no! There he goes using all of that trader jargon—calls, puts, straddles, strangles, and so on." No worries; in this book it's all about speaking plain English. We will learn what calls are, and all the other trading terms, later.

All of these commodities and many more are almost certain to experience intense volatility heading into and during hurricane season. But keep in mind that volatility drives the commodity markets.

The fear of what *may* happen can be more of a factor than the actual storms, so it's best not to be greedy. Use a hedge for what it's for: protecting your overall portfolio from the losses other holdings in your portfolio and property may take as a result of the storms.

Another thing about hurricanes is that they do a lot of damage and leave a mess to clean up. In 2005, more than 113 oil platforms were destroyed and over 400 pipelines were damaged. Sometimes the best way to play resources is to buy equities related to the companies that harvest the resources as well as provide the drilling equipment and, eventually, the transportation of the finished goods. For example, while not a direct resource play, buying stocks related to transport of oil workers from oil platforms and terminals was a very good investment that year. Even heading into the 2006 hurricane season it proved fruitful. Smaller stocks in companies that transport workers to and from rigs and facilities—specifically, boat and helicopter companies— were a very good investment. This play was good globally, too. In the Scottish newspaper *The Scotsman,* Frank Urquhart wrote about it just prior to the hurricane season in 2006 ("Copter crisis threatens oil industry," 6/30/05):

> North Sea helicopter companies are struggling to meet a surge in demand for their services because of a shortage of aircraft and crews to fly them, it was revealed yesterday.
>
> The soaring price of oil has led to a sudden and major increase in helicopter operations in the offshore oil and gas industry.

Helicopters and transport are commodities in their own right in times of need. This is only one example of the many investment opportunities available that are simply associated with the commodities themselves. Shipping, rail, storage, you name it—if it hauls, plows, ships, builds, or refines, we can relate it to commodities and it can be a profitable addition to our portfolios.

BEYOND THE STORMS

It can be as important to understand the psychology of the markets as it is the mechanics. At the start of hurricane season nobody knows for sure just how bad it will be. One thing is certain, though—a lot of attention is being paid to it. This can often have the reverse effect on a trading market should the hurricane season be relatively light. The old adage "Buy the rumor, sell the news" certainly applies here.

In other words, put your positions on early and take early profits simply on the back of the fear of what might happen, not what actually does happen. Being married to a weather position is never fruitful for a portfolio. Simply get in and get out. A smart trading strategy would be to add one or all of the vulnerable commodities; then as you enter the season, with a bit of luck, grab fairly quick profits, even before the first winds start to really hit. There are many different scenarios—at least as many as there are weather patterns—and we will address them more thoroughly later. Remember, timing is everything. It's always important to be four to six months ahead of the regular calendar when trading commodities. Keep in mind that we're trading futures not "currents"; it's vital always to be looking forward and thinking about the impact of news, weather, and geopolitical events months in advance.

A VIEW FROM THE INSIDE

Another thing this book will do is give you an insider's view of what actually goes on in those trading pits and show you some of the tricks of the trade. The market's strange terminology can be a big hurdle to traders new to commodities. Words like *hedgers, speculators, locals, scalpers* all sound a lot more mysterious than they really are. Each commodity has its own particular jargon, and once you learn it you'll be well on your way to a better understanding of these markets. Here's an example: "The locals were short the Dec/Jan softs across the board. They used limit orders and GTCs before the commercials came in and the funds, too."

Huh? Don't worry; in this book I will always speak in plain English and teach you what much of that jargon means, demystifying it so you don't ever have to feel intimidated again. The language of the markets is very important to know, whether or not you ever actually use it. I'll help you learn, so that you will feel like a pro. By the way, here's the translation—let's break it down:

The locals in the pits. The "pits" refers to the trading pits where all the trading takes place—you know, that wild, frenzied place you sometimes see on TV. The "locals" are traders who usually trade only for their own accounts; they play a vital role in the markets by providing liquidity. Without locals, it would be much more difficult for the huge players—the major banks and institutions—to move into and out of the market efficiently. *Short the Dec/Jan softs across the board.* First of all, "softs," or "tropicals" as they are sometimes called, are commodities such as sugar, coffee, cocoa, cotton, orange juice, and even lumber; "Dec/Jan" just refers to a spread trade between the December and January contracts. "Across the board" is simply all the softs. "Limit orders" and "GTCs" also are called *contingency orders;* they simply place a limit on what you will pay or ask for a certain trade. GTC stands for "good till cancelled" orders. *Commercials came in and the funds, too.* Commercials and funds are institutional buyers or sellers and can often be a strong fundamental indicator of a market's direction. Is your head spinning yet? I know it all sounds confusing, but by the end of this book I guarantee it will all be a lot clearer and you'll be tossing those terms around with the best of them—and understanding them, too!

Once you've seen how these markets function, how locals in the pit work, what those strange-looking order acronyms and alphabet soup mean, which markets are thinly traded and tightly controlled, and so on, you'll feel much more confident and better able to jump right in and grab those profit opportunities that are just waiting for you.

FUNDAMENTAL TECHNICIANS AND TECHNICAL FUNDAMENTALISTS

Like stocks, commodity prices don't always go down or up. But the one thing you can practically guarantee about the commodities market is that somewhere prices are on the move. And predicting these prices is where fundamentals and technicals come in.

Technicals versus fundamentals, which is better? This is an ongoing argument among traders, but actually they're *both* necessary. I use both technicals and fundamentals, and I firmly believe it's vital to have a well-rounded knowledge of both in order to be a successful trader. The trick is to know when to rely more on one or the other, or sometimes even neither, and just go with your intuition—your gut. Sometimes, for some of us, this is the best indicator of all.

Certain commodities, such as crude oil, tend to make use of the fundamentals; others, such as financials, rely more heavily on technicals. As I talk about different commodities in this book, I'll show you how these two methods can be used to build your own trading system around these markets and make solid profits.

RULES OF THE GAME

My major rules regarding discipline and trading are a constant theme in this book; in fact, I can say that my success is due in many ways to discipline tempered with flexibility. I talk about trading rules and the pitfalls of breaking them. You'll see examples of how discipline paid off and not only kept my profits high and intact but allowed me to sleep at night. You'll also see how, in some instances, my lack of discipline burned me—a perfect opportunity for you to learn from my mistakes.

Human beings, I believe, are fundamentally morbid. (Ever notice how many gapers slow down or even stop when they see a car accident on the freeway?) Consequently, one of the most common questions I am asked is "What is the worst mistake you have ever made trading?" Now, most people are being polite when they ask that; what they mean to say is "What is the most money you've ever lost in one day?" The worst trading mistake I ever made was not necessarily the one that cost me the most money. It was in 1991, before the first Iraq war. To make a long story very short, I was long the U.S. dollar index futures, in a far bigger position than I should ever have had, but I knew it was going to go higher once the war started—I just knew it! Famous last words.

The night the missiles started flying over Baghdad, the dollar did just as I had predicted—it rallied big-time. So I went to bed thinking I was a genius and was all ready to cash in my millions the next day. Wrong! As the night progressed, it was obvious that there was not going to be a long, drawn-out battle, and that the United States was already in almost full control. The dollar did not just drop, it sank like a stone all night long. Without getting into all the horrific details, I had broken about 10 of my trading rules, and I paid a heavy price. Sure, the financial price was heavy, but it was more the psychological damage that was done to my trading psyche that bothered me. It took me months to recover and not to be overly cautious and second-guess myself. As traders, we all need rules and guidelines to be consistent; otherwise, we are all only one trade from oblivion. So heed that occasional wake-up call—you probably need it!

COMMODITIES BOOM

It's almost impossible to turn on the business channel or read the financial pages these days and not find a story about the next commodity that's breaking an all-time price record: crude oil surpassing the $74 mark for the first time ever, gold and silver at 25-year highs, copper surging to record levels, and sugar, too. It's enough to make a trader's head spin. Suddenly the technicians are all scrambling for more paper or a bigger screen so they can fit the chart on the page. We're seeing many of these commodities in truly uncharted territory.

In market conditions like these the most important thing an investor can do is remain focused and disciplined. One of the classic mistakes investors make in these types of volatile markets is to become greedy and lose sight of their objective. *Don't do it!* It's one thing to have a price objective and quite another to "talk your book" (floor terminology for a trader who speaks positively of a market based on his or her own trading position, regardless of what the market is actually doing; it's also known as *denial*). When I was in the Dollar Index pit a long time ago, one trader, whose name I will not mention, always talked his book. He was short U.S. dollars, and as more and more good economic numbers came out he talked more and more about how well he was doing. One day when I got to work he was gone and all his trading accounts had been seized. Now that's some serious denial.

Risk management in any trading strategy is one of the most important tools and the most often overlooked. Risk management falls right into the same category as discipline; without it, most traders lose money consistently. A solid basic risk management strategy encompasses clear entry and exit levels, using stop orders and limit orders and, most of all, never getting emotional about the trade. This can be the toughest challenge for many traders. Passion is different from emotion, in my opinion. When I get passionate I get energized; when I get emotional I can make bad decisions. So my advice is to detach yourself from your trades somewhat; when they go against you, don't take it so hard, and when they're in your favor, don't let your ego run away with you. The two "E"s, emotion and ego, can be a deadly combination.

It's also important not to go with the herd. "The trend is your friend" is an important and oft-used saying, but the motto traders use more often instead is "The trend is your friend, until it ends." Take a chance and look away from the crowd for an unpolished gem or a market that isn't as active—you may be surprised at what you find!

CONCLUSION

In this book I will show you what you need to learn to have a working understanding of what really goes on in those chaotic trading pits and how you can make it work to your extreme advantage. I will share with you my own pitfalls and successes so that you can build on them without having to endure all the pain. I will show you how to take huge profits from movements in markets you've only heard of but were afraid to trade, thereby succeeding beyond your wildest dreams. As I've said before, the commodities markets are the last bastion of pure capitalism on earth, and now you're invited to the party. Are you ready?

CHAPTER 2

ENTERING THE PIT

MY TRIAL BY FIRE

It seems that everyone, at one time or another, asks you, "What was your major in college?" When I would answer, "Philosophy," people would often look puzzled. Quite frankly, I felt the same way. I mean, what do you do with a philosophy degree anyway? The listings for philosophers in the want-ads section are thin at best. Funny enough, years later I would come to find out that many of my colleagues in the trading and publishing businesses had been philosophy majors, too. So I guess law schools, trading floors, and publishing houses are where former philosophy majors end up.

Anyway, I graduated from the University of Southern California with my shiny new philosophy degree and promptly left for Europe for three months with my best friend. When I got back, I realized that my already strained student budget was even more threadbare. I had no desire, nor the LSAT score, to attend law school. But I was fond of eating. One day my friend Tim Butler mentioned to me that his brother David needed an arbitrage clerk on the trading floor. I said, "What trading floor?" This question changed my life.

Up until that point the only exposure I'd had to commodities was back when I saw the movie *Trading Places.* I truly didn't know livestock from preferred stock. Well, when I asked what an arbitrage clerk did, my friend said, "I don't know, but he'll pay you $22,000 a year." Now, for someone just out of college without two nickels to rub together, $22,000 a year sounded like a great job.

So there I was on a warm August morning in New York City, ready to launch my career on Wall Street. I headed downtown on the number 4 train, cramped as always, decked out in my best suit and tie. I got off at the Fulton Street station and took the short walk over to the World Trade Center. There I searched for 4 World Trade Center, which housed all four New York exchanges at the time: the New York Mercantile Exchange, COMEX for the precious metals, the Coffee Sugar and Cocoa Exchange (CSCE), and my destination, the New York Cotton Exchange.

The six-story black building was dwarfed by the Twin Towers, and few noticed the buildings that sat at the base of the towers. I found the elevators and pushed the button for the fifth floor. It was very early— around 6:15 AM. I was eager to make a good impression. Unfortunately for me, nobody was there yet. As I got off the elevator, the first thing I saw was the letters "CEC" directly on the wall in front of me. They stood for Commodities Exchange Center. I walked up to the guard and he looked at me strangely as I told him I was here and was going to be an arbitrage clerk in the Dollar Index.

He must have thought I was nuts, dressed in a suit and tie and trying to get in at 6:00 AM. He took pity on me and issued me a visitor's badge and told me I would need to get my credentials later. He then directed me to the entrance to the trading floor and said that nobody was in yet but I could go straight through that entrance. I headed over that way; the quiet darkness inside intrigued me.

As I approached the top of the entrance I could hear the hum of all of the equipment. There were numerous television monitors; some telephones were ringing, but most just had red lights flashing above them. Ticker tapes (electronic ones) on the walls were flashing quotes and news into the dark, empty room. I remember in the darkness hearing a big thump every once in a while. Later I found out it was the time-stamp clocks—hundreds of them—making the loud thumping noise. The monitors hung from large poles in the center of the trading pits. The pits were all different sizes and shapes; the majority were octagons, but some, like the orange juice pit, were just circles with a wooden ring. The room itself was cavernous—almost three stories high, I found out later—although it was so dark that I couldn't really tell then. I remember the floor was very clean—not one bit of paper or anything else. I wouldn't realize how clean it was until later in the day.

When I found my way over to where I was supposed to be meeting David Butler, my friend's twin brother, I sat down on the edge of the pit and just looked around. Suddenly the lights came up and it was as if someone had turned on the sunshine in a huge stadium. Now I could see just how big this trading floor was. It was enormous—like nothing I had ever seen before.

PLUNGING RIGHT IN

Even though I had no clue about what to do, I was put straight to work. I was shown where the phones were. Then I quickly took off my jacket and tie and was handed a trading clerk's jacket, green with blue trim. Our clearing firm was Gelderman, and green and blue were their colors. Anyway, I was quickly shown that the phones didn't ring; even if they did, you couldn't hear them, so above each phone was a light. The lights indicated the phone was ringing, and when it was busy all of the lights were flashing. This was when I realized that I had stumbled into no ordinary job.

The Dollar Index market was a small pit with about 50 people, if that. To me at the time, it seemed like a very tiny, crowded space. People were coming in with their multicolored trading jackets, holding their trading cards, and nobody really said much—certainly not to me. I was instantly initiated into the fraternity once the bell rang and the frenzy in the pit began. I was overwhelmed—the noise, the kaleidoscope of multicolored jackets, the sheer volume of paper everywhere, all made my head spin.

When the closing bell rang at the end of the day I felt as if I had been through a war. Most of the time throughout the day I'd had no idea what was going on and I felt totally lost, but I stuck it out. I remember a trader, whose badge read "GAMA," asking me, "Are you coming back tomorrow?" He must have seen the forlorn look on my face. But come back the next day I did, and every day since. And while I wouldn't trade (pardon the pun) my experience for anything, I hope that throughout this book I can help you learn and understand the commodities markets from an insider's perspective without having to go through all the turmoil I did (unless, of course, you want to!).

WHY SHOULD ANYONE LISTEN TO WHAT I HAVE TO SAY?

I'm sure I asked this question at first when my visionary publisher, multibook author, and friend Addison Wiggin, of Agora Financial, first approached me about writing this book. After all, I freely admit my writing style and my direct approach are a far cry from those of many financial writers. I'm not the type to try to convince you to accept a great theory of trading; I'll leave that to others. I'm more of a straightforward, no-nonsense kind of guy who believes you learn by doing, or by having the tools to avoid the mistakes others have made.

Some of my colleagues on the writing end think of me as simplistic and in the beginning probably even thought of me as just lucky. That changed with time. Truthfully, I'm no genius—but I am a hard worker. Hard work and passion make up for a shortage of genius, I believe. The old saying (it's on one of my coffee mugs) is "The harder I work the luckier I get."

IF YOU BELIEVE, YOU CAN ACHIEVE

Truly, anything I've ever wanted to accomplish, I've done. I wanted to move to New York when I was 16 and be an actor on Broadway. People laughed—especially my family—but I did it. I wanted to go to New York University; I was told I wouldn't get into the film school, so I went in as an actor and left as a philosophy major (I transferred to USC). I wanted to become one of the youngest members of the New York Cotton Exchange; I was told it wouldn't happen, but it did.

I wanted to start my own business and write successful trading newsletters to help others. My friend Tim thought I wouldn't succeed, but he believed in me enough to let me use office space in his law firm. Two years later I sold that business and started another million-dollar concern. I wanted my own column with a respected news organization, and suddenly I had it with Dow Jones.

I started doing television around 1999 and then a few years later I decided I wanted to be on national TV regularly. It took a lot of work and a lot of people told me it was unlikely, but now you can catch me on TV almost every week. I'm interviewed by radio stations and newspapers all around the world. Finally, I wanted a lovely wife and a child, and I've been blessed there, too. All of it is from hard work and a genuine belief that no matter what, I can do anything I put my mind to.

I'm telling you that the two things a successful trader must have are willingness and determination. This is not something that I or anyone else can teach you. In this book I'll give you many of the tools you need to feel confident and knowledgeable about trading, so that you'll feel ready to go out and achieve whatever *you* want to with *your* trading.

The biggest impediments to trading are negativity and self-doubt. As a trader, you may sometimes question your skills, decision-making ability, and so on. This is especially true when losses mount, and suddenly you go from hero to zero. Actually, it's not so extreme. It's important to keep yourself and your ego right-sized. Don't beat yourself up when you have a loss and don't pat yourself on the back every time you turn a profit.

As I write this in late 2006 some of my positions are against me. It happens even to the best of us! However, if I look at my track record for the last 12 to 16 months, it's amazing. You must always see the big picture. Don't be a wishy-washy trader. Develop specific rules, actions, and disciplines, many of which I'll teach you in this book. Don't be swayed by the herd. If you're consistent, you'll be way ahead of the pack.

THE MANIAC TRADER'S INVESTOR'S OATH

I'm truly convinced that great traders overcome the psychological obstacles (and there are many) that impede most people from being successful. To be successful yourself, it's important to understand some measure of psychology and what has helped make great traders succeed.

It's a fact that more than 50 percent of people who try to trade commodities consistently lose money. Why is that?

Some of the answers can be found in the writings of Jack Schwager, author of the popular Wall Street book *Market Wizards: Interviews with Top Traders* (Collins, 1993). Schwager talks about managed investing, but his theories can apply to individual investors as well. He writes:

> In our experience, investors are truly their own worst enemies. The natural instincts of many lead them to do precisely the wrong thing at the wrong time—with uncanny persistence! Managed futures investors are no different. At the heart of many a typical investor's blunder is his or her tendency to commit to an investment right after it has done very well and to liquidate an investment right after it has done poorly. The problem is that many investors first wait for the CTA in whom they've expressed interest to prove himself before jumping on the bandwagon. Compounding this error, they then abandon ship during the first rough period, even if the account hasn't yet reached the originally intended bail out point.

More than 17 years of observing and working with investors has led me to believe the wisdom in the words of Jack Schwager.

It's important to psychologically prepare yourself before trading such speculative markets as commodities. While it may sound a little weird, even taking an oath is a good idea.

MY INVESTOR'S OATH

I've picked up many tidbits over the years, and one that I like is from the Investors' Credo; I'm not sure who the original author is, but I cut out a lot and I ended up with the Maniac Trader's Investor's Oath:

Risk and volatility are the price I must pay for riches and opportunity. I don't want to lose my investment, but the capital I've invested is risk capital I don't need to live on, and my lifestyle wouldn't be affected if I did lose it.

I will have realistic expectations. Even the best of traders are only human, and can look their worst when losing. I don't expect to have only winning trades, and realize that losing trades are just as integral a part of my performance as are the winners.

I realize that an investor's emotions can be his or her own greatest enemy during drawdown periods. I will not allow myself to be victimized by my emotions like so many other investors. I refuse to be part of the herd!

I will think with my head and not my heart! I will stick to my original investment game plan that I agreed to when I opened my account. I will have patience, think long term, and stay tough! I'm not a fair weather investor.

There it is—learn it and try to live by it. I do.

STANDING APART FROM THE CROWD

The clear-cut difference between professional traders and everyone else is their method and discipline—and this is the reason for their success. The methods they use encompass all the system trading knowledge, rules, discipline, and market knowledge that have been garnered over the last 50 years or so.

These things are not some major secret that only I and an elite few know about. They're available to anyone, yet most investors overlook it all. However, many of the things I'm going to teach you in this book are detailed and specific, and they are generally not available outside professional circles.

Ironically, nonprofessional traders have completely the wrong idea about how the professionals trade. This lack of understanding is the breeding ground for rumor, false belief, and wild stories. It also provides a good foundation for unscrupulous people to develop products and ways in general to confuse and often intimidate investors—especially to trap the novice or overeager trader.

The techniques of professional traders go a lot deeper than just being methodical; they incorporate a knowledge base that's been built up over years of experience. These methods aren't complicated, but they are detailed, and they have to be applied with discipline and consistency.

This can be a major problem because most of us are not good at discipline and consistency. Learning by personal experience is usually very expensive—especially so in commodity trading—which makes it even stranger that most people choose to go this route.

I want to clearly outline why professional traders make the majority of the profits in the commodity markets. I'm aware that these reasons aren't well understood and that they have nothing to do with the myths that most new commodities traders think are responsible for their success.

I concluded that the best way to find an answer would be to cast my mind back to the time I began trading and ask this question: *What did I really need to know when I began trading commodities that I later found was essential for success?* Here are my answers:

- How to identify those markets that are of use to *you* and those that aren't.
- Why *your* trading goals are not the same as those of the next person and why they are much more than just targets.
- How and why discipline and flexibility are vital to success.
- How the professionals turn what appear to be moderately successful systems into multi-million-dollar winners.
- Where do I go from here—what is the next step?

Right now, you're standing at the place I refer to as the *enlightenment barrier.* All new traders must pass through this barrier before they can begin to make progress with their trading. In this book I'll help you get through this initial barrier and create a good foundation of knowledge for you so you won't feel so confused. This is the first step.

The markets are very dynamic, and you may experience success and failure as a trader. Focus on the learning aspect of the markets and develop a relationship with a reputable and helpful broker that will assist you in your trading. In sum, patience, discipline, education, and consistency are all important qualities to cultivate in your trading. Good luck!

CHAPTER 3

NOT YOUR GRANDFATHER'S (OR EVEN YOUR FATHER'S) COMMODITY MARKET!

A nasty rumor has been going around that the commodity markets are old hat and will soon go the way of the dinosaur. "They" have been saying that since I started on the floor almost 20 years ago. I'm here to tell you that not only are these markets stronger and more modern than ever, but there's never been a better time than right now for investors like you to make lifestyle-changing profits, and probably more quickly than you ever thought possible. I know, because I've done it myself!

The most common question people ask when they find out I'm a commodities trader is, "So how are pork bellies doing?" Pork bellies (bacon, for the uninitiated) are one of the old-timers of the commodity markets, along with corn, soybeans, wheat, cattle, pigs, lumber, and gold, not to mention silver, foreign currencies, government debt, and eurodollars. Many of these have been around for decades, even centuries (in the case of the grains). And many more that were popular at one time (eggs, butter, potatoes, frozen tiger shrimp) no longer exist. For example, back in the late 1980s, when I started out, they used to roll out a blackboard on the floor of the exchange and trade butter futures one day a week, I think. The actual excitement was from the side bets on how long the market would actually stay open, not on the trading itself. You see, it stayed open only if there was an active bid and offer within a certain period of time. However, at one time butter was a very important market—now it has been reduced to little more than a joke. This happens all the time in commodities; certain markets fall out of favor while others rise. It's the natural selection of the markets— market Darwinism, if you will. Also, many commodities can seem to die but then come roaring back to life again.

Soybeans are a good example. Some people call soybeans a miracle crop because they're found in everything from tofu to floor cleaners and crayons to animal feed. They've certainly been a miracle for the U.S. farm economy! In 2003, U.S. farmers harvested $17.5 billion worth, accounting for 16 percent of all U.S. crop production and second only to corn in value. Today, as biofuel comes on the scene and the world market for soy products explodes, demand for soybeans is projected to increase exponentially by 2007. But there was a time when the soybean picture didn't look too rosy. In 1974, the world produced 701 million bushels of these miracle beans; by 1997, world production had more than doubled, to 1,597 million bushels. In April 1997, soybeans were trading above $9 a bushel; four years later, they traded at around $4.20 a bushel—less than half that price—for a 25-year low. Was this commodity staple dead? *Wrong!* In the summer of 2002, prices broke out of a three-year bottoming formation as high export demand from China and drought conditions in the United States resurrected the soybean from oblivion.

What happens when prices and demand for commodities run high over time? Lots of money gets reinvested into making more of that commodity. Pretty soon, you've got more of the resource than you need, just sitting in storerooms. Or how about hot demand that gets so hot there's a correction? Prices for that resource plunge. And again, we make money simply by capitalizing on those moves.

Over and over again, the cycle keeps playing out over time— especially today, with resource prices trading on more exchanges and more quickly than at any time in history. This may be your best chance in a long time to get very rich very quickly.

Over the last decade the commodity markets have changed to the point that to some they may be unrecognizable. Since 1848, the open outcry and hand signal method of trading on commodity exchange floors was the only way to go. Enter electronic trading in the early 1990s, and soon the old auction method looked as if it were about to die any minute. Add the Internet and easier access to these markets by individuals, and it was bye-bye trading floor, hello computer screen. We all know that didn't happen, and I personally believe it won't happen. But we can't deny that the electronic era is here to stay. We're going to talk in depth about the electronic markets and how to use them to your trading advantage in Chapter 9.

Today's trading methods aren't your grandfather's, and neither are today's markets. The markets we see actively trading today may not be the only ones we will see trading five years down the road. We may see alternative energy commodities such as ethanol take off from their infancy. We may see markets like corn and sugar explode because of ethanol demand. We may see new contracts for such things as water.

We've seen commodity exchange seat prices jump, and we've seen the world scramble for resources. The explosion in commodities and natural resources over the last few years has been remarkable. As a nearly 20-year veteran of these markets, I have never seen anything like it—and it's showing little sign of slowing. Here are some of the commodities that I see as hot in the future.

FIRST, THE OLD STANDBYS . . .

There are certain commodities that are staples of trading and most all investors should know these sectors and be very comfortable with them.

Gold Rules!

"All That Glitters"—that's what the old COMEX marketing line was. Back when I started trading, the COMEX was the top exchange in New York, the crème de la crème. The badge was green in color, and it took a lot of "green" to get one. At the time, a seat on the COMEX also was the most expensive seat on the New York exchanges, of which there were really four: the Coffee Sugar and Cocoa Exchange (CSCE), the New York Mercantile Exchange (NYMEX), the New York Cotton Exchange (NYCTN), and the Commodities Exchange (COMEX). Chicago markets like the Chicago Board of Trade (CBOT) and the Chicago Mercantile Exchange (CME) were viewed as being on an even higher plane, and most Chicago traders considered the New York markets to be second-class citizens. Now much of that has changed. But as I arrived on the scene, a pivotal shift was happening: As the NYMEX began to grow in stature, the COMEX became a bit more tarnished.

The Hunt brothers' silver debacle, after their attempt to corner the world silver market in early 1980, drove many investors away from the metals, and some never returned. Today, however, the metals have come full circle, and silver, which for most of my career traded in the $5 to $7 range, is now busting out to new highs almost monthly. For many years, gold was simply a hedge against inflation, but not anymore; today, the shiny yellow metal is being sought as a flight to a quality instrument but also for its uses in jewelry on a large scale. The new gold exchange-traded funds also have helped to drive the price of gold higher, as these new instruments are backed by physical gold.

E-gold is another phenomenon that is not just fantasy anymore. Gone are the ideas of returning to barter using gold nuggets. Today's modern commerce allows the exchange of electronic gold credits between parties all around the world. This virtually eliminates currency risk and opts for one currency: *gold!*

The metals markets can be very volatile, and one strategy for capitalizing on the long-term rise in gold is to use options—specifically, long-dated gold options that may seem very far out of the money. FYI: An option is the *right,* but not the obligation, to buy or sell something (called the *underlying*—in this case, gold futures contracts) at a specific price, before the expiration date of the option. A long-dated option is one that expires a long time into the future. For example, as I write this, gold is trading in the low $600s but has been over $700 an ounce. It's quite possible gold could surge to $1,000 an ounce, and any traders worth their badges would want to be in on it! So to play this right now (with gold at $623), we would add the $950 call options. They would be considered quite far out of the money.

There's one of those pesky trader terms again. Let me clarify. In dealing with options, when you buy an option and the current futures price is below your option's price, it is called buying an *out-of-the-money* option. When the futures trade up to the price of your option, it is called an *at-the-money* option, and when the futures price is above your option's price, it is called an *in-the-money* option. As I was saying, a $950 call option would be considered way out of the money if gold was currently trading at $623, but all that could change if gold rallies to new highs.

Meanwhile, by buying gold options, my risk potential is limited to the premium (price) I pay; I can't lose any more than I initially invested. It is one of the safest ways to invest in gold. (Again, many of the terms in trading options sound complicated but actually aren't; simple definitions for many terms are included in the Glossary of this book.)

Every Portfolio Needs a Silver Lining

For years the silver market has languished in a narrow range with little momentum and not much of a bright future. Unlike its golden counterpart, silver has been more like the redheaded stepchild of precious metals. Not anymore.

This often maligned metal is up a whopping 60 percent since the beginning of 2005, and so far 2006 is looking good, too. There are many ways to play silver, just as there are for gold: silver bars, ingots, coins, jewelry, certificates, stocks, futures, and options. All have advantages and disadvantages, but the one we want to add to our portfolio is silver options.

Silver closed at its highest level in more than 22 years recently on hopeful expectations that the Securities and Exchange Commission would soon approve a silver-backed exchange-traded fund. This silver ETF is similar to the gold futures-based funds, streetTracks Gold and IShares Comex Gold Trust. According to reports, investors hold more than 14 million ounces of gold in the ETFs—that's significant because it's equivalent to about a fourth of last year's worldwide supplies. In 2006, silver had an incredible performance in my portfolios and those of my readers. The launch of the silver ETF drove silver prices up several cents, and seemingly out-of-the-money options were tripling and quadrupling in price. In less than a two-month period, our positions were returning unheard-of 400 percent profits and went even beyond that.

Heavy Metals

Platinum and palladium fall into the realm of ultraprecious metals. These metals are important for jewelry, but they also serve some key industrial purposes. Platinum and palladium are used in things like catalytic converters, flat-panel TVs, and electrical circuitry. Now, don't get me wrong, platinum and palladium are two markets I rarely have traded, and I will tell you why. They're expensive! Margins for these contracts are very high, and these markets also are also extremely volatile. I truly never expect to see the type of liquidity that exists with gold in the ultraprecious metals; they are a class unto themselves. Let me give you fair warning that, although ultraprecious metals can yield tidy profits, you must make sure you know what you're trading and how much it costs. This rule holds true for all markets.

With great risk comes great rewards. Palladium futures gave me a tenfold return in a matter of weeks in 2005. While these markets aren't for everyone, there are incredible opportunities to be found in them.

Energy

Opportunities abound for investors in the energy market right now, just looking at what's being set in motion globally. The end of the age of oil will not be a disaster if we are prepared for it as investors and consumers. Acceptance is the first step.

Aside from water (more about that later in this chapter), the world is most thirsty for oil. Since the last major oil crisis in the 1980s, there's been tremendous population growth, with no less than one-third of that population beginning to industrialize their economies. Look at China, home to 1.3 billion people, and India, with more than another billion. Both these economies are growing fast, and they must have oil. Then add the United States's oil addiction to the mix, with our ever-larger gas guzzlers and our seemingly insatiable desire for bigger and better, whether it's cars, boats, houses, amusement parks, shopping malls, or whatever.

Combine this demand with dwindling global supply, the ongoing threat of terrorist attacks, the fact that there has not been a major oil find in more than 36 years, natural disasters such as last year's hurricanes along the Gulf Coast, and continued geopolitical tensions, and don't be surprised if oil reaches $150 a barrel, or more. How can you capitalize on this?

It's always important to have vision, to see beyond the short-term outlook and predict what can and may happen in the future. It's essential to know which seasonal and geopolitical factors will drive demand. Do your homework! Learn to decipher and understand industry reports such as the Energy Information Agency weekly inventory report. By using spread trades and options in the energy markets, traders can maximize profit potential while limiting downside risk. (Spread trades are exactly what they sound like. The most common spreads are those between the different trading months, such as December/January spreads or, as we call them, Dec/Jan spreads. Basically, you are simply trying to trade a price differential between the months. There are many different types of spreads but this kind is the most common.) Seasonal plays in the energies and other strategies we will talk about later also offer solid investment solutions.

Oil is the lifeblood that moves things, that keeps the whole world functioning and growing. In the last 100 years we have become very spoiled—we've been used to easily obtained, easily moved, and easily processed petroleum, crude oil, and natural gas. We have simply come to expect that they will be there forever, or at least for our lifetime.

Oil, among other things, spurred the development of the internal-combustion engine, which does the work of a thousand people. Oil essentially constitutes a major workforce throughout the world.

This virtually invisible workforce has allowed the world's population to grow to over 6 billion. Not only that, it has allowed us to plow millions of acres of land, to produce fertilizers, to transport people and goods, even to wage global wars and to set up global communication systems. Our dependence on oil, and energy as we know it, is similar to an addict's powerful affliction. The world's craving for oil is just as debilitating.

A Future for Coal?

At this moment the United States doesn't have an energy source that would be as easy to produce and transport as oil. Nuclear power can produce electricity, but the remaining rich uranium ore will last for decades, not for centuries. Renewable energy can probably never cover the current levels of global energy consumption or even U.S. consumption. So what is a practical solution right now?

Recovery from oil addiction is possible, and the long-term, easy-to-reach answer may be in a fuel source that is right under our feet—coal. Coal is cheap and reliable and much cleaner-burning than it used to be. As the world goes through painful withdrawal from oil dependence, coal may help. It seems that the market feels this way, too: Coal prices have been soaring over the past year.

Clean coal technology (CCT) is employed when coal arriving at a power plant contains other by-products that need to be taken out before it can be used. A facility like this uses a number of processes to remove unwanted minerals, which makes the coal burn cleaner and more efficiently.

Coal has often been stereotyped as a dirty and less desirable product of the energy industry, but not anymore. As the world searches for energy solutions, coal is at the forefront, and new, clean-burning coal technology means it's highly likely that coal will be around for some time to come.

Where's the Beef?

A year ago, the average choice grading steer fetched around $85.50 per cwt to the meat packer. (The abbreviation "cwt" stands for hundredweight. Hundredweight simply means "per 100 pounds specified weight." It is always qualified as the type of weight used for cattle.) Two weeks ago, the average was $94.44 cwt, an increase of $3.32 over the previous week. Translation: Prices for cattle in the cash market are climbing fast and they will most likely continue to do so. Demand is the driver.

As more countries reopen their markets to U.S. beef, demand will increase. Meat packer margins are hovering at break-even levels. Right now, tight cattle supplies and plentiful inexpensive feed will likely result in a firming up of the cattle price. This holds true especially for cattle producers and feedlot operators.

Then, of course, there's avian flu. If one case of bird flu migrates to the United States and infects one person, people will swear off poultry and head right to the meat aisle in the supermarket. In reality bird flu is not actually spread by eating poultry, but often in trading perception is reality and just the threat of bird flu is enough to get the general public to shun poultry. Even though eating it isn't the cause of the illness, the general public won't differentiate. And who would want to bite into a chicken of death when they could opt for a nice juicy steak? *What* mad cow? Typically, market participants have a short memory, so it's important to act on fear while it's still in full swing. The cattle and meat markets in general are the butt of many jokes in the investment world—Hillary Clinton's infamous cattle trade comes to mind, as does the aforementioned question about pork bellies. Truth be told, the meats are a good agricultural market with solid fundamentals and can be a great learning market for the novice trader—just make sure no one knows you're a novice.

In 2006 I carried October live cattle positions and made some very good profits on the 86 call options, and later on the 88 call options. The cattle market is a volatile one and relatively illiquid, so it can be a difficult market if you're just starting out. You may want to avoid it until you get some experience.

Coffee, Sugar, Cocoa, Cotton, Orange Juice

The coffee, sugar, and cocoa markets are near and dear to my heart. These three commodities are also known as the *tropicals,* because most grow in the tropics, or *softs,* I guess because they're all soft in texture. But whatever you want to call them, these are some of the best-performing and least understood or talked about markets. I spent much of my early career running between the pits of the coffee, cocoa,

OJ, and sugar markets, and let me tell you, these are markets that trade like no others. Gold and oil may get the lion's share of the sound bites and headlines, but if excitement is what you're looking for, these markets have it.

Sugar, for example, is one of my favorites. It is growing exponentially in demand as a result of ethanol production and being widely used in foodstuffs; meanwhile the supply is shrinking due to factors such as European subsidies being curtailed. Sugar is likely to double in a couple of years, in my opinion, and the writing is already on the wall.

Much the same can be said for markets like cocoa and coffee. Worldwide demand is sucking up supplies faster then these commodities can be harvested. I know the coffee market well—very well, in fact. It's one of the first markets I traded when I started out in commodities 18 years ago. It's also one of the fastest-moving and most volatile markets, which means it's loaded with opportunity for you to make a lot of money. This is a good example for talking about one of the best features of trading commodities: the ability to short a market just as easily as going long. That's correct—unlike equities, you can short commodities futures just as easily as going long. A market like coffee is particularly important because of its volatility but also because a new Starbucks pops up on every corner from Maine to China and every farmer who could possibly grow coffee beans is doing so, resulting in a glut of beans on the market. Even Juan Valdez, from the TV commercials, hung up his sombrero in 2006. Coffee is thus one of those markets you can play from both directions to get maximum profits—something futures allow you to do, with astounding results.

Cotton gave this maniac trader his start. My first full seat was on the New York Cotton Exchange (now the New York Board of Trade). My badge was 8015 QUEST, as in Jonny Quest. (I was young and had blonde hair and a dog named Bandit; when the guys on the floor found out I had done cartoon voiceovers as a kid, the name just stuck. Everyone gets a nickname down there, and it usually isn't something you'd choose for yourself.)

In any case, cotton is an "old boy" market, much like cattle or the grains—not old as in stale, but old in that it has been around a very long time and the people who trade it have been doing it a very,

very long time. Cotton is a great market to trade, but you must understand the fundamentals at work and the differences between *old crop* and *new crop*. This simply means that two different cotton crops are produced each year in cotton, and you must make sure you know which crop you're looking at and then make your decisions based on that. Cotton is one market that's crucial not to underestimate and, much like the ocean, never turn your back on. Trust me, I worked in there for a number of years.

Right next door is another very active market, especially in the winter and during hurricane season: orange juice.

Orange juice is a perfect market for learning about fundamentals the hard way. Many of you have seen the movie *Trading Places,* with Eddie Murphy and Dan Aykroyd. If you haven't seen it, do—it will give you a good laugh. The movie was filmed on the old World Trade Center trading floor and was about trading OJ, but the reality stops there (or does it?). Actually, with tongue in cheek, I can say that it's probably a fair depiction of the old trading pits.

Today, however, the OJ market is tightly controlled by supply and demand and is certainly ruled by weather factors—not just winter hard freezes, either. It may surprise you to know that hurricanes in Florida are the biggest factor influencing this market, not only before the hurricane hits but after, too. The main concern is citrus canker; after the winds and rain die down, this fungus can develop on the crop. Fundamental information like this is important to know and take into consideration when initiating a position.

Soybeans, Soybean Oil, and Soybean Meal

Every market is different, so you must study the fundamentals for all of them. For example, you must understand what soybean meal is used for as opposed to soybean oil.

Soybeans are used for biofuel, among many other things, so nowadays soybean prices more closely parallel those of crude oil and heating oil than those of the regular crop reports.

Keep in mind that these markets move on the basis of supply and demand. Right now, the demand for soybeans is picking up in a big way due to biofuel consumption, which in turn relates to how high heating oil prices are. It's not hard to connect the dots to identify what affects a specific commodity, but sometimes you've got to do a little research first. Biofuel is used primarily for home heating, and as ethanol is derived from corn, biofuel is derived from soy. The bottom line is that you must know, inside and out, the basics about whatever commodity you choose to trade, whether it's rough rice or natural gas. More important, you need to know new factors that may affect a particular market—and these can change.

SOME NEW ENTRIES INTO THE COMMODITY CLUB

Never Before in History Have We Depended More
on Electricity

It turns our turbines and runs our assembly lines; it powers the Internet, our databases, and company networks. When we read in bed, turn on the air-conditioning, look at the nighttime skyline, it's there. And we take for granted that it will always be there, every time.

But when more and more people, in more and more countries, start making that assumption, you have a situation. Right now, one in every three people doesn't even *have* electricity. And already, our electrical grids are overtaxed and electricity demand is higher than it's ever been.

What happens when the *rest* of China and India hop onto the power grid?

In China alone, electricity demand is 150 percent higher right now than it was when China first started to boom, back in 1980. Worldwide electricity demand is expected to explode by another 85 percent before the year 2020, faster than demand for any other kind of energy.

What happens when the world population hits 7 billion? How about 8 billion? Or 9 billion, as the United Nations is predicting?

Hospitals without life-support machines. Grocery stores without refrigerators. Shopping malls, office towers, and neon gone dark. Printers and fax machines that don't hum. Trains that don't run, phones that don't ring, computers that don't blip or announce new e-mail. . . . because there is no e-mail; there is no Internet. The global grid is down. And where it's still up and running, it's pockmarked with dead zones that have made the whole network slow to a crawl. Even the electronic stock tickers on Wall Street have flickered out.

Without billions of dollars invested in new *electricity* resources right now, imagine brownouts, blackouts, shutdowns, and worse on a scale 10 times greater than anything we're seeing today.

This all sounds scary and not quite real. It doesn't have to be real if the biggest and most ambitious economies in the world kick in right now with several hundred billion dollars to jump-start a whole new era of electricity investing.

The good news is that the total $16 trillion headed for all the energy markets—including the $10 trillion that will go into electricity— is still just a *fraction* of the total global gross domestic product (GDP)—only about 1 percent. So making the investment is not only very possible, it's nearly certain.

The electricity markets are still in their infancy in the commodities world. As with so many other up-and-coming opportunities, you just have to be ready to seize those chances when they come. Speaking of opportunities, alternative energy is another area investors are focusing on, and one of the biggest is solar power.

Here Comes the Sun!

The idea of using the sun to solve the earth's energy needs is hardly new; it's been used since the dawn of time. What is new is the technology and research money that are breathing life into the industry. The rallying cry for quick and easy solutions to our nation's oil addiction spurred immediate interest in alternative energy, from nuclear to ethanol. Solar power faces some challenges, to be sure, but there are some solid players who certainly bloom in this sector. Just add sunshine and a little ingenuity, and watch the profits grow.

Solar Power Is Shining Brighter

Since the 1970s, the solar power industry has come a long way. We've reached a point where solar power is no longer a gimmicky, peculiar energy source; it's now more of a necessity.

The solar energy industry has made enormous progress in the past

20 years, finding new solutions to the ongoing problems of high costs and massive regulatory barriers—but there are still roadblocks.

Solar technology has become more affordable, due mainly to higher demand and the goal of eliminating dependence on foreign oil. Manufacturing processes have been streamlined and continue to become more cost-efficient with the help of government subsidies, consumer rebates, and tax credits.

As oil prices continue to increase exponentially, it seems inevitable that a convergence of the cost of conventional and alternative energy costs will occur. Many companies in the solar sector seem to be focused on the development of improved solar efficiency through broad-based applications that can be put to practical, immediate use.

Now, one thing that is very important to investors in any sector is the fact that every trade has flaws. In the case of solar power, there are several.

Forecast: Partly Cloudy

Although there is so much good news for solar power, there are challenges, too. For example, there's the lack of silicon, which is needed for making solar panels. A silicon shortage has limited the supply of the panels and frustrated potential buyers. Orders take several months to complete, and prices, after years of floundering, have increased by as much as 15 percent.

The real winners are those companies that benefit from the lack of silicon, primarily producers of less efficient, yet available, thin-film solar panels. Of course, other beneficiaries include companies that have emerging technologies, such as plastic solar cells.

Worldwide, the solar market has exploded, growing by 40 percent annually in just the last five years. Germany and Japan alone use 39 percent and 30 percent, respectively, of the global solar panel stockpile. The United States is a distant third, at only 9 percent of the global solar panel supply, according to various energy information sites. California is likely to drive that stat much higher as demand grows exponentially in that state and others, too. As we focus on the sun, let's turn our attention to another key element on the opposite end of the spectrum, one of the most precious commodities on earth: water.

Water, Water Everywhere . . . Not!

One of the most valuable commodities on the planet is water. Safe, drinkable water is difficult to find in many places on earth. Demand is surging for nature's most important resource. Yes, oil is important, but not as important as staying alive—after all, you can survive only about a week without water, right? Just look around. How much water do you personally use in a day? And think about how much water you don't even realize you use. Water is something we take for granted, and it's a growing crisis that's beginning to hit traders' radar screens.

Reports from the World Health Organization show an epidemic problem: A staggering 2.6 billion people—40 percent of the world's population—do not have even the most basic sanitation, and more than 1 billion people still drink unsafe water. This can cause a range of diseases and even death. The world is just one natural disaster away from a lack of clean water. One example of the devastating impact of nonpotable water was the tsunami in Asia. Many thousands of deaths could have been prevented had there been fresh water supplies.

Water pushed through hydroelectric dams is one of the world's most efficient and harmless forms of electricity generation. Water is also vital in sanitation, manufacturing, drinking, and more. The water industry is very complex. The list of related companies is long, from water suppliers and bottlers to technology and equipment firms.

Portfolio Soaked with Profits

Think there's no real way to play water supply and demand? Think again. The explosion of the world's population and the dwindling supply of fresh water on the planet are sounding alarm bells for the greatest commodity play of all time. Make no mistake: Water is an increasingly vital commodity. And that hasn't gone unnoticed by worldwide capital markets.

Very few people know about the Dow Jones U.S. Water Index. This index lists only 23 companies, mainly utilities, but rest assured that there are many, many others. Surprisingly, many experts contend that the way to play water isn't just through U.S. utilities. Worldwide, the utilities are considered overvalued to some extent.

Even though the utilities are expensive in the United States, one country that offers even better opportunity due to pent-up but exploding demand is China. China's population of 1.3 billion is more than one-sixth of the world's total. The sheer numbers are staggering. And while not everyone there drives a car, everyone does drink water.

Watershed of Facts

Here's a list of water crisis facts, provided by Summit Global Management:

- The World Health Organization says that 60,000 children die each day from lack of water and/or dirty water, by far the largest health problem in the world.
- Only 20 percent of the world's population currently enjoys the benefits of running water.
- Every year, according to the World Bank, the amount of global water polluted equals the amount of water consumed: Fresh water is disappearing at an alarming rate, especially when compared to the rising world population.
- Since the turn of the last century (1900), the U.S. population increased 200 percent, while per capita water usage shot up 500 to 800 percent, depending on the region.
- It takes 1,000 tons of water to produce 1 ton of grain; agriculture consumes 75 percent of the world's fresh water. The World Water Council says we will be 17 percent short of necessary water to feed the global population by 2020.
- Users of the most water in California, in decreasing order, are alfalfa growers, cattle ranchers, cotton farmers, rice farmers, and the city of Los Angeles.
- In the United States there are 58,000 water utilities, 90 percent of which serve less than 4,000 homes and have operating budgets of less than $2 million.
- About 500,000 tons of pollutants pour into U.S. rivers and lakes each day.
- California accounts for 20 percent of all irrigation and 10 percent of all fresh water use in the entire United States.

Opportunities exist in the United States, if you pick the right players. The U.S. water infrastructure, much like the oil refinery situation, is falling apart. The Environmental Protection Agency (EPA) and others estimate that up to $1 trillion will have to be spent to upgrade U.S. water infrastructure over the next few years. That work will fall into the hands of only a few key players in the water market, and the rewards for the shareholders of those that are chosen could be substantial. It's unclear as I write this which players will be on top in the next decade; some may not even exist yet, but will be born out of necessity. As I mentioned earlier, the best thing to do is to keep an eye on China, as their need for water will be the most immediate. Take, for example, the grain situation in China in summer 2006. Severe drought afflicted China's poor western region and underscored how vulnerable the country's critical ecology was despite its growing wealth, raising concerns among some big commodities traders that China might need to import massive amounts of grain.

A report by the United Nations Food and Agriculture Organization warned in 2006 that some parts of key provinces lost half of their winter wheat crops. Some areas experienced massive food shortages that were on the verge of epidemic.

The cause was lack of water supplies—an ongoing and growing problem in China. In some villages and cities the major water sources have reportedly dried up by more than 70 percent, according to the UN agency's global information and early warning service.

China was the fourth-largest destination for U.S. farm products in 2006, overtaking the European Union, with purchases of $6.8 billion, according to the U.S. Department of Agriculture.

It seems ironic that millions of Chinese are potentially facing food and water shortages, even as the nation's economy is growing by leaps and bounds. That growth clearly comes at a price worldwide, not just in China.

Speaking of prices, we continue to pay an ever-higher one for our energy. The boom in mining, drilling, foresting, and other resources sectors has a downside, too—a negative effect on our environment. From greenhouse gases and strip-mining to deforestation and drilling in Alaska, the commodities boom is not without casualties.

Energy and mining are on the top of the list when it comes to harming the environment. Just ask anyone who lived in Alaska when the Exxon *Valdez* disaster occurred. The ecological implications were daunting. Drillers and the oil majors are spending more and more to protect the environment, partly for public relations and partly because they have to. However, measures are being taken in some sectors to stop the destruction—and this is also providing an opportunity for investors.

Various companies that do cleanup and reclamation are set to do well as an ecology-conscious world demands that we be good stewards of the environment at the very same time we are searching for resources. Investing in these companies is a way to further expand a winning portfolio.

CONCLUSION

The commodities markets are always in flux, and it's important to keep up with new markets and new opportunities. *Never* judge a book by its cover. I remember in the stupidity of my youth being offered a natural gas seat to trade on the exchange for free. For free! I turned it down. You see, the badge was purple and my cotton badge was orange and if you own both, it makes your trading badge half purple and half orange, so I said no.

Seriously, I said no because I didn't believe a natural gas contract would ever be successful. After all, the commodity was tightly regulated and it comes through a pipeline controlled by spigot. Well, chalk this one up in my loser column; I know when I get to heaven and they are reviewing me for entry, this one will come up as one of the more foolish decisions of my youth. Today, natural gas is a highly liquid and sought-after seat; I won't tell you how much the seats go for. You just never know what the next hot thing is going to be, but it may be the thing you least expect.

Always study the markets you want to enter—take an interest in them. One of the most important things in this business is to be interested in what you are trading. Otherwise, trading becomes a chore. I personally don't trade Treasuries—why? Not because they're not good markets but because they don't really engage me. Others couldn't care less to trade sugar; I, on the other hand, am passionate about it. That's the key: Be passionate about the market you choose to follow, but *never* let emotions cloud your judgment. I will explain in detail later why it's so extremely important to have trading rules and discipline and to stick to them.

CHAPTER 4

SECRETS OF A FLOOR TRADER— REVEALED!

THE INITIATION: KEEPING THE SECRETS
UNDER LOCK AND KEY

Freemasons would be considered a fairly open society compared to
floor traders. While there are no secret handshakes or strange pass-
words, the world of the exchanges is one unto itself. Maybe not as
much today as 20 or 30 years ago, but the veil of secrecy still exists.
No, I don't mean shady dealings or crooked schemes. I mean the
secrets of how much money can be made trading commodities and
how easy it can be to do it.

So you may be asking, "Why would they want to keep it a secret?"
Obviously, the fewer people who figure out what a good place the
markets are to make money, the more there is for those players. By
keeping secrets, they exclude the masses from the riches to be made.
In the past, the floor traders rarely hired outsiders; normally they
would hire family and friends to work in their floor operations.

Back when I started, the only way you could get a job down there
was if you knew someone who worked there—a father, an uncle, a

brother, a cousin, or a very best friend who considered you a brother (this may sound sexist, but there it is); that's how I started. Today the attitude on the trading floor is much more open; in fact, nowadays even CNBC cameras are on the trading floor occasionally! We see a younger generation of floor traders, past and present (yours truly included), opening up and actually welcoming investors to understand and use these markets.

The commodities markets are continually evolving. They have stripped away much of the old secrecy from days gone by that, in my opinion, kept many investors at arm's length, which was not a positive thing for the markets in the long term.

JOINING THE CLUB: MEMBERSHIP HAS ITS PRIVILEGES

Like any other society, club, or membership organization, the commodity markets have their own rites of passage. I'm often asked how I got my start in the business. My story is not all that unique; as I told you in Chapter 2, I got my job from my best friend's brother, David Butler.

In June of 1989, armed with my shiny new bachelor's degree from the University of Southern California, I had no clue about what I wanted to do for a career. After all, there aren't a lot of job listings for new philosophy graduates! Anyway, I tossed around the idea of going to law school but had no real desire. Having moved back to New York after graduation, poverty was setting in fast, along with the grim reality of being in the cold, cruel world. That's when my best friend's brother Dave offered me a job with him and his other brother, Thomas, down on the floor of the New York Cotton Exchange.

As I said earlier, if you had gone to one of the major trading floors in the United States in the 1980s, you would have found that most people worked there because they had a friend or a relative who gave them a job or they knew someone in the industry. While today it's not anywhere near what it was in the 1980s, there's still a strong old-boy (or -girl, now) network in this business. There are always a few outsiders who come in because they have a lot of money. However, in these situations, it's rare that they survive long, unless they bond with the other people in the pits. Because most of you will never have a need to actually trade on the floor, what I'm telling you may seem irrelevant, but trust me, it's not.

If you're going to trade commodities profitably, it's vital that you understand the inner workings and psychology of the market participants, as well as what actually goes on in the pits. By understanding what goes on in the pits and with the floor brokers, as well as with your own broker on the trading desk, you'll be able to empathize with them and know when to ask for more and when to ask for less. Knowing what your brokers can do for you and what is beyond their power makes them appreciate you and consider you an ally. It puts you on their favorite clients list—not a bad place to be. It's always a good idea to have your broker like you because he or she will look after you better. While all ethical brokers should, and generally do, do their best for each client, chances are that they would go above and beyond what's expected of them if you take the time to establish a rapport. You don't have to move in together, but just show that you're making an effort to understand what they do and how they do it. The best brokers will call you when they see an opportunity—or, in other cases, a problem—with your account. They will be quicker to do this if they like you. They can tell you what trades are simply not a good idea, help you understand terminology and even decipher the various industry reports, and a lot more. Even better, brokers like clients who have a basic understanding and try to learn the workings of the market. When you have that understanding, you have an instant edge over the vast majority of novice commodities traders.

DOS AND DON'TS

In any business, you always can tell the novice from the pro, and the commodities business is no different. Some of the most important lessons to learn and some of the most common early mistakes a new commodities trader makes fall into a few categories. I alluded to these at the beginning of the book, and now we'll take a closer look.

Mistake: Not Having a Clear-Cut Trading Plan in Mind for
Profit Objectives, Maximum Drawdown, and General Strategy

Everyone wants to make money, obviously, but the way most traders approach the markets, you wouldn't know it. The first thing traders should do once they enter the market is place a stop order—not always an actual, real-life stop but at least a clear-cut mental one. Traders should know in absolute terms how much they're willing to lose on a specific trade; then, if it isn't going their way—bang! They place a stop to protect the position. For example, each time the market moves a point in December crude oil, it's worth $10.00.

Now, how did I figure that out? Simple—I looked it up, and so can you. All commodities have a per-point or per-tick value (a *tick* is the smallest increment of price movement possible in trading a given contract), which is known as the *multiplier*. For example, crude oil's tick value is $10. Each commodity is unique. Sugar is $11.20 per point, cotton is $5 per point, and so on. Getting back to crude oil, remember that it's $10 per point or penny. Confused? Don't be. Think about it: Crude oil trades in dollars and cents, so if you're in long (you've bought) at $72.08 and it trades to $72.09, you just made $10; if it trades to $72.10, then you've made $20, and so on. So if you were long from $72.08 and want to protect yourself to a loss of $500, your stop should be at $71.58 (which is $.50 on the downside). Simple, right?

Mistake: Not Taking Profits

The second mistake—and in my opinion, an even worse one—that most traders make is that by not taking profits, they get greedy. Why wouldn't you take profits when given the opportunity? In other words, if the crude oil market moves up to $72.58, that's a $.50 profit, for a total gain of $500. The trader could exit the crude market, taking his or her profit off the table, and then jump back in when presented with another opportunity. Most of the time, however, they don't. The reality is that most people hold onto the position until it turns around and they are losing so much they are forced to liquidate. Avoid this at all costs by setting your goals from the start, by grabbing gains, and by not being greedy.

Another way to play it if you have multiple positions is to simply liquidate one of the contracts and hold the other. In other words, if you buy two contracts you can sell one as the market starts to go up if you're long. Then as the market, as hoped, goes even higher, you would sell the other one. An even smarter move is to take your protective stop order and keep moving it up behind you as the market moves higher. Eventually the stop will be above where you initially entered the trade, and even if the market reverses itself you will likely be stopped out with a profit or minimal loss. Bravo!

So if you were holding onto two contracts or positions in December crude oil from $75.00 and the market rallied to $75.50 and you sold the first contract, you would make $500. Then if the market continued higher to $76.00, you could sell the second contract for a profit of $1,000. Nice!

Mistake: Not Moving the Stop with the Market
to Protect Profit

Let's illustrate with a trade in sugar. Say we buy an October sugar futures contract at $15.44 and then we set our sell stop order below the market at $15.00. Now the market moves higher, to $15.95. Our smartest strategy is to move our stop up now from $15.00 to our entry point of $15.44, or breakeven. In other words, we would break even on the trade, more than likely. Later, if the market moves even higher, we can move the stop again, and now almost guarantee a profit. This type of activity is called *placing a trailing stop,* because it trails behind our trade and moves as the trade moves. This is smart trading. Master it, and use it.

Mistake: Letting Losses Run and Taking Small, Quick Profits

This is one of the worst mistakes new traders make (I know from vast, often painful, experience in my youth). I remember playing the game of hoping my Dollar Index positions would turn around when I was first starting out in the trading pit; they rarely did. Wishful thinking is not a good trading strategy—being disciplined is. Not having a well-thought-out game plan and strict trading rules is truly a recipe for failure.

Often new pit traders in particular will get hit hard and then become overly cautious. They resort to taking small profits even though those miniscule gains might have turned into a large profit that could have offset all their losses if they had just been a little more patient.

I still find myself tending to let losses run rather than doing what I know is right and getting out of the position to reevaluate. As I mentioned in Chapter 1, it's all too common for traders to talk their book, or live in denial, hoping against hope that the market will turn their way. This is almost guaranteeing that it won't. Traders in the midst of losing tend to live on the misplaced hope that the market will retrace and then let them break even. Instead, this mentality actually leads to the opposite and creates even bigger losses. The markets can be cruel, and they seldom come back or retrace to let you off the hook. All of this can be avoided or dealt with quite easily. Simply use discipline and, more important, predetermined stop orders to prevent your losses from closing your account. Equally important is to have a plan to take profits at a very specific level and stick to it.

Lesson: It's Important to Look at the Big Picture

If Trader A makes 20 trades of which 15 are winners and 5 are losers, and Trader B trades 20 of which 15 are losers and only 5 winners, who in your mind has won? Well, duh! The answer's pretty simple at first glance. But not so fast—we have to dig deeper. How much profit did Trader A make on those 15 winning trades compared to Trader B and his gains from his 5 transactions? Also, how much did each lose on his respective transactions? In other words, Trader A may have more winners than losers, but at the cost of losing most of his money in the process, while Trader B may have more losers, but his winners may be much larger.

Mistake: Greed and Lack of Discipline

These are the two biggest hurdles new commodity traders face, and overcoming them is a long and ongoing process. Contrary to Gordon Gekko's famous (or infamous) line in the film *Wall Street,* greed is *not* good. In fact, in this business it could be lethal. How do you overcome these tendencies? Well, life on the floor is kind of like living in a big support group: not always pleasant, and certainly not always good for the ego!

When I was getting my feet wet and was still green as grass, I was surrounded by traders who had been in the pit for a very long time, some since the founding of the exchange. And believe me, they were the first to let me know when I messed up! A cardinal sin in the pits is to bid into someone's offer. In other words, when you step into the pit, you announce yourself. Usually you simply shout out the month you're trading—for example, SEP or OCT (September or October).

Then people in the pit will yell back something like "2 bid at 8." That means they are willing to pay 2 or sell at 8. It's just an indication, but it gives you an idea of where the market is. To bid through someone's offer means that if I entered the pit and bid 9 when they were offering at 8, it would be a very big no-no. And they let you know about it! So I only did that a couple of times before I wised up. Either you learn quickly down there or you're out, no two ways about it. Those people who beat me up for that stuff are the very same ones who taught me the valuable lessons I needed to learn to trade these markets on and off the floor with incredible success.

By having experienced people around you or within your network you can find support and advice that can prove invaluable. Building an information and trading network can make implementing and adhering to trading discipline far less cumbersome and more enjoyable. Nobody will help you enforce your own rules—that's each trader's private responsibility—but a good network often can tell us as traders when we may be on the wrong path or simply talking our book. How do you build a network? In today's world, it's not hard at all.

As with everything in life, it's good to have friends in the right places; one commodity that I value above almost all others is my network of traders. I developed this network over the years by communicating with people across all areas of resources and commodities, from floor brokers in New York and Chicago to resource companies in Canada to other traders in Internet chat rooms and at seminars.

The old saying that "two heads are better than one" is right on the money. Before I make a move into any trade, I get a feel for market sentiment by checking in with my network. Now I don't rely entirely on them, not at all. I don't always consult with them, but if I want another opinion I can always get one. As a writer, I get thousands of e-mails a month, which help to give me a clear picture of what market participants are thinking and doing, and that can prove invaluable, too. You may not get thousands of e-mails (if you're lucky), but chat rooms and other sources can be good places to see what others are thinking.

Fatal Mistake: Self Will Run Riot

Emotions, good or bad, are of little benefit to the commodities trader. Overexuberance at a good trade and feeling suicidal when a loss occurs serve no purpose. Wins happen and losses happen, and a trader needs to stay level-headed and focused, or be consumed by the market frenzy.

The phrase "married to a position" is used when someone has a losing position and won't let it go, no matter what. Take my advice— get a divorce. When you see a position isn't working out as you expected, get out of it. Being married to a position means you're not being rational and looking at the trade objectively; you're letting your emotions get in the way. *Don't do it.* Go back to the reasons you initiated the trade in the first place. If the situation has changed, the best advice may be to change the position, too.

Liquidity and Open Interest: Two Vital Ingredients

Two major factors a successful trader must look for in any new trade are liquidity and open interest. Liquidity simply allows us to more effectively enter and exit the market; a liquid market is far safer to trade and exposes us to less price volatility. Open interest is an indicator of just how liquid a market is by showing how many open trades are in any particular contract. This can be especially important when trading options, so as not to get stuck in an option with very little activity. Like a roach motel, you will get in but you won't get out if it's illiquid. Remember, higher open interest equals better liquidity. More liquidity means a more competitive market, and a more competitive market means more opportunity for you to make money.

BREAKING DOWN THE BARRIERS

Before we talk about avoiding newbie mistakes, let's do a quick review.

Navigating the Basics

Futures contracts are standardized, legally binding contracts traded through regulated exchanges; the exchanges are "meeting places" where individuals gather to conduct business. And even though more and more futures contracts are traded online, there's still plenty of action in the trading pits at the various exchanges.

An investor agrees to buy or sell a fixed quantity and quality of a certain commodity at a specified price for delivery in the future. The customer's funds are placed with a registered commodities dealer who is required to keep these funds separate (in segregated accounts) and not use them for any other purpose than the intended investment. The regulatory agencies that oversee these activities and markets are the Commodity Futures Trading Commission (CFTC) and the National Futures Association (NFA).

Commodity futures are unique because they're traded in what is known as *open outcry,* or auction-style, trading. Buyers and sellers meet and trade in an area often referred to as a *pit* because the space usually resembles a small depression, or pit. Traders scream and yell to get *pit recognition,* and buy or sell their contracts at the best price. The price action can seem chaotic but is actually well orchestrated and extremely efficient. This is truly organized chaos on a grand scale—market professionals conducting business at lightning speed either for customers or for their own profit. In markets where prices move rapidly over very short periods of time, the speed of trade execution and timely delivery of orders to customers is vital because every minute (or second) that goes by can mean a huge difference in how much money is gained or lost in a trade.

How do traders know what price is fair or a good investment? Futures prices change constantly, responding to many factors, including breaking news, inflation, labor strikes, weather, economic forecasts and reports, political events, foreign issues, new technology, and even

---

ELECTRONIC REVOLUTION

Electronic trading is one area we must address because this is the wave of the future, and it's already here. Pit trading is romantic, but chances are, most of you will never need to be concerned with too much of what goes on in it day to day. Most major commodities markets can be traded electronically, and more and more are every day; some electronic markets are accessible 24 hours a day around the globe. The Chicago Mercantile Exchange's Globex® system was one of the first used to trade currencies; there are many others now and they all go by different names. The principle is the same, though.

The important thing to know about electronic trading is that unlike in traditional pit trading, orders are not executed in a trading pit but are matched up by computer at lightning speed. As the markets evolve, traders are embracing the electronic trading platforms, but the trading pits will likely never disappear completely. We'll talk more about electronic markets later in the book—much more indeed—because they are so important in today's global economy.

---

rumor. It's been said that futures markets are often the scene of original price discovery, because so many buyers and sellers are interacting with bids and offers, which lead to the best measure of the actual price for the commodity. Even so, these markets can be full of risks, so it's important to identify them and know how to handle them. The factors that affect prices can change at any time, and anyone who claims to guarantee profits in a commodities deal with little or no risk involved should be completely avoided. That guy who claims to "know absolutely" what will happen with the weather, geopolitical risk, or whatever, is not the one you want to do business with!

Do What the Big Boys and Girls Do—Avoid Risk

One risk factor stems from the *leverage* inherent in futures contracts— the relatively small amount of money (known as *margin*) that is needed to control a large quantity of the commodity you're trading.

Leverage is awesome because even a small change in the price can cause a large change—upward or downward—in the value of a futures contract. For example, in the case of a crude oil contract, a $1 move translates to a $1,000 gain or loss for the futures investor. The downside of leverage is that an investor can lose more than the initial investment if market conditions make it impossible to liquidate or offset the contracts. Unlike stocks, commodity futures have maximum daily trading limits. These limits are preset and, when reached, halt all trading for that session. When a market continually trades at the limit, this is called *lock limit*. This can happen for several days in succession and make it almost impossible to get out of a trade until it has gone significantly against the trader.

Another major risk in futures trading, or in any form of investment—and the most avoidable, in my opinion—is the risk of doing business with a dishonest or unethical individual or firm. It's absolutely vital that you perform due diligence before opening an account or seeking advice. Today, this is easier than ever. There are so many resources, especially the Internet, from which one can seek out testimonials and complaints as well as regulatory information on individuals and firms.

Check out your potential firm's history and find out whether they have any complaints against them. This can be done as easily as going to the NFA web site at www.nfa.futures.org to determine whether a firm is registered to conduct futures business. You can check out individual broker history there as well.

Remember, the NFA is the self-regulatory organization for the futures industry. Another good approach is to check with your local Better Business Bureau to see if the firm has a history of customer complaints. More good information sources are your state or provincial securities administrators, the federal Commodity Futures Trading Commission, or your state's attorney general's office.

For as many bad apples as there are out there, 10 times as many totally ethical and helpful brokers exist. I have found that word of mouth is the best source of information. Visit chat rooms and see who other people use and what their experience has been, and then ask a lot of questions. This is a good way to meet other investors and at the same time build your own network.

Key Questions to Ask Your Potential Broker

Always ask a lot of questions—remember, there's no such thing as a stupid question. Often, people end up blinded by profit potential without really understanding what they're getting into or whom they're dealing with. Step back and take a breath. Be patient and quiz the firm that is selling commodities. See whether they know their stuff. Never go with a wishy-washy or uncertain broker who won't answer questions such as these directly and fully:

- Are they registered with the CFTC, NFA, or any other regulatory agency?
- Do they conduct transactions to be executed through a regulated commodity exchange?
- Does the firm have literature or written materials explaining the transactions or a risk disclosure statement?
- What is their fee rate and margin policy?
- How long has the particular broker been in the business and what is his or her NFA ID number?
- How long has the firm been in business and who are its principals and officers?

If anything seems fishy or not quite right, then it's probably better to move along to the next candidate. There are hundreds, if not thousands, of highly qualified commodity trading advisors (CTAs) and brokers, so shop around before you make that important decision that could change your life.

The other most important factor is how well you like this broker's personality. Hiring a broker and bringing him or her into your network is a little like getting married. Be sure you're going to enjoy talking to and interacting with this person and that you trust and respect the person. After all, your broker is going to be your lifeline to the trading pit; you want someone on your side who will look out for you and alert you to profit opportunities on a regular basis. A good broker also can advise you on which markets are thinly traded, when you should use stop orders, and similar issues.

Which brings me to another major mistake traders can make early on: trading in illiquid, or "thin," markets. This can be very risky. A thinly traded market is one in which there are not a lot of participants. This type of market offers little liquidity and is trickier to move in and out of, making it more difficult to offset a position. So it's better to avoid such markets unless you're absolutely sure you have the skill and experience to handle them. Illiquid markets that come to mind are the ultraprecious metals like platinum and palladium, natural gas, lumber, and cattle, to name just a few. Just because a market is thinly traded doesn't mean you can't make money; in fact, quite the opposite is true. It's just that you will have to assume much greater risk tolerance, swallow a lot more Rolaids, and get a lot less sleep at night.

While we're speaking of thinly traded markets, another person I hope you never have to get to know too well is the margin clerk.

There's a Reason for Margin

Margin. Few words conjure up more fear in commodity futures than that one (except maybe *tax audit*). But in all honesty, margin is a good thing. Unlike in the stock market, margin in commodity futures acts as a performance bond, ensuring that a trader will meet his or her obligations. When you initiate a commodity futures position, you usually only put up an initial deposit of about less than 10 percent of the value of the position; you then must maintain a specific amount in your trading account while your position is open. Your initial margin requirement is relatively small compared to the value of the position, and the resulting leverage can lead to quick and substantial profits (or losses). Keep in mind, though, that it's possible to lose more than the amount of money you've deposited. A good rule of thumb is to use only funds that you can afford to lose without affecting your ability to pay the mortgage and eat regularly. Furthermore, devote only a part of these funds to any one trade.

If the market moves against you, you run the risk of experiencing the dreaded *margin call.* Enter the margin clerk, who has the unenviable task of informing clients that a position has gone against them and that they must replenish their margin accounts immediately. (Yes, there are people who actually want this job, believe it or not! Go figure.) When a client receives a margin call, the margin clerk will give the client a certain period of time to meet the obligation or have the position(s) liquidated. If possible, get to know the margin clerk at your brokerage firm, preferably before you experience a margin call. Don't get me wrong; it's not going to get you any special treatment or extra leeway, but it will give you a relationship ahead of time, and the margin clerk will be more keen to give you time to meet the call and be fair, rather than treating you as just another account number.

Brokerage firms have one goal: They want zero risk. Know your firm's margin policy thoroughly and be sure to meet any margin calls should they arise. The best practice is to use strict stop order discipline to avoid getting a margin call in the first place. A skilled, full-service broker who is worth his or her salt can teach you this, and while the commissions may be a little higher, the knowledge you gain can pay for itself a hundred times over.

Learning from History: The Market Often Repeats Itself

The truism "History repeats itself" likewise applies to the market. Anyone can try to predict commodity prices and statistically have a fifty–fifty shot at success. But price forecasts are just the first step in the price decision-making process. The second and often more difficult step is market timing.

As with so many things in life, timing is everything in the commodities markets. The difficulty lies in the fact that because futures markets are so highly leveraged (as mentioned earlier, initial margin requirements are generally less than 10 percent of a contract's value), minor price moves can have a dramatic impact on trading performance. It takes exact timing of entry and exit points to maximize profits and minimize losses.

To perfect their timing, many traders use technical analysis extensively. They utilize charting principles, which become absolutely essential in the price forecasting and risk determination formula.

Technical analysis is founded on three basic principles:

1. *History repeats itself.* People are predictable, and science can prove it. Psychology therefore plays a big role in technical

analysis of the marketplace. Human behavior patterns have been identified and categorized for centuries. The repetitive nature of the marketplace and people is most clearly evident from specific chart patterns that indicate a follow-through or a change in trend. The old saying "The trend is your friend" is usually right.

2. *Trading trends.* Most of the time, prices can move in one of three directions: up, down, or unchanged. Once a trend in any of these directions is in effect it usually will remain constant for a period of time. All a market trend really is, after all, is simply the movement of market prices, which, as I said earlier, is the key to the success of technical analysis. Figuring out trends actually is quite easy, and yet many traders turn it into some advanced science. By studying a simple historical price chart, you can determine the prevailing trend by a series of waves with obvious peaks and valleys.

   The direction of these peaks and valleys makes up the market trend. There are multitudes of different variables, and for the number of people from whom you ask advice on this subject, you will get as many different answers. History, however, can be a good teacher for both fundamental and technical study; never discount it.

3. *The Wave Theory.* If you are a technical type of trader, then you should be familiar with the Elliott Wave Theory, which interprets market actions in terms of recurrent price structures. In a nutshell, wave theorists believe market cycles are composed of two major types of wave: the impulse wave and the corrective wave.

   Every impulse wave can be subdivided into five-wave structures (1-2-3-4-5), while a corrective wave can be subdivided into three-wave structures (a-b-c). See Figure 4.1.

Waves within Wave

An important feature of Elliott Waves is that they are fractal in nature. This means that market structures are built from similar patterns on larger or smaller scales. Therefore, we can count the wave on a

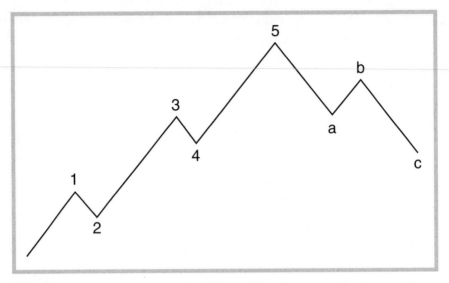

Figure 4.1 Each impulse wave is subdivided into five wave structures, while a corrective wave is subdivided into three (a-b-c).

long-term yearly market chart as well as on a short-term hourly market chart. See Figure 4.2.

Rules for Wave Count

Figure 4.2 looks like an erratic heart rate monitor, doesn't it? It's not that complicated, really. Based on the market pattern, we can identify where we are in terms of wave count. Nevertheless, as the market pattern is relatively simplistic, there are four rules for figuring out the count:

1. Wave 2 should not break below the beginning of Wave 1.
2. Wave 3 should not be the shortest wave among Waves 1, 3, and 5.
3. Wave 4 should not overlap with Wave 1, except for Waves 1, 5, a, or c of a higher degree.
4. Rule of alternation: Waves 2 and 4 should unfold in two different waveforms.

It's a little cumbersome to use this system and it's not for everyone, but you should at least know what it is. The thing about wave theory

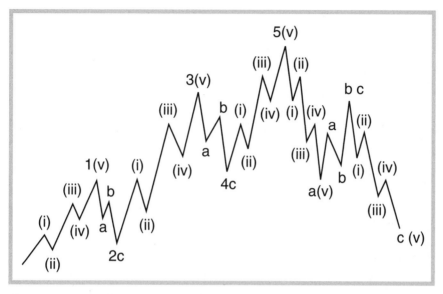

Figure 4.2 Wave formulations can seem erratic, but there are very specific patterns and rules.

is that it can be a bit too subjective for me. In other words, you can tweak it to fit your own trading outlook, in my opinion. But never discount these patterns in the market, if only for the reason that many players in the market are looking at these exact same patterns and acting on them religiously.

HISTORY LESSON: THE MORE THINGS CHANGE, THE MORE THEY STAY THE SAME

In the 1970s, the United States experienced strong export demand combined with a major drought in the Corn Belt. These two factors caused commodity prices to soar to a level that was way beyond any previous market price. It was a winning lottery ticket for farmers who could supply good crops. There are stories of farmers who bought new equipment every two years. They lived the good life, taking lengthy, expensive vacations every year, and still could not spend all of the money.

(continued)

Fast-forward to when the government took steps to wring inflation out of the economy in the 1980s and the scenario changes dramatically. Property prices surged as the land became a financial anchor when interest rates skyrocketed to double digits and crop prices plummeted. Those same farmers who were living high on the hog were the first to be slaughtered. Those who had had all the money and spent it on expensive assets that did nothing to increase cash flow fell into the vicious trap of borrowing based on the artificially inflated value of their land. Ironically, farmers in the areas affected by the 1970s drought did better than those who were living the good life during the boom. The main reason was that they hadn't overextended themselves with credit and borrowing, and their relative poverty ended up saving them.

It took several years of restructuring and the liquidation of assets at deflated values before the financial situation improved by 1988. We all remember the Farm Aid concerts and the farm auctions—it was not a pretty time at all.

You would think that after all that, farmers would have learned the hard lessons taught by the tough times in the 1980s. But they didn't. Now, as we enter the new commodity boom, prices for many of the major commodities are reaching historic levels and some of these patterns are repeating themselves. Only time will tell if the same mistakes will happen in the agricultural arena again. One thing is clear, though—we are still only at the start of the commodities boom cycle.

In my view, traders who survive and thrive in these roller-coaster situations are most conservative when conditions are good and least conservative when times are bad. If you look at 1929, the people who became wealthy were those who had the presence of mind to buy while others were jumping out of windows. This applies to commodity trading, as well to the rest of farm management or any other venture. It is also completely the opposite of human nature. It's normal for people to view current conditions as lasting forever; of course, they never do.

If prices are booming, we spend without end. If prices are in the dumps, we hoard and groan that finances will never improve. Actually, neither viewpoint has ever been true for very long. A smart trader who knows history has a good chance of seeing ahead of the curve and thus making smart, profitable trading decisions before others even realize that history has repeated itself, and will continue to do so.

SIFTING WHAT TO PAY ATTENTION TO AND WHAT NOT TO: FILTERING OUT THE NOISE

Sometimes when I turn on the TV and listen to the commentators talk about commodities, I cringe. For years the media treated commodities as a secondary asset class or, worse, a form of legalized gambling; to some extent they still do. Their understanding of how the markets actually function is rudimentary at best. Now, I'm not saying these journalists are not intelligent—some of them are brilliant. They just don't understand how the commodities markets work. Yet they have such power that when the camera light goes on, millions of people hear and believe what they say. Having participated in a lot of television and print media myself, I know that they can be very powerful tools, but as they say in the *Spiderman* movies, "With great power comes great responsibility."

Let me be clear—I make use of the media and information superhighway every day. I have colleagues who are deep philosophical thinkers and don't even own a TV; however, I have five computer screens in my office and two televisions. Does this make me nonphilosophical and obtuse? No, because most of the time I keep the volume down on the TV, which improves my IQ immensely.

Distractions of any sort when trading can be of little or no value. The TV blaring opinions that change moment to moment can be one of a trader's most useless tools. A friend and colleague of mine— we'll call him Jack—used to work in the office across from mine. Jack is one of the best currency traders I know, and he and I come from the same mold. Jack never had a TV in his office; he thought it was worthless and that what was said was mostly drivel. For the most part he was right. More important, Jack's point was that TV offered him nothing beneficial for his trading—it only interfered with his system and was a distraction; in other words, it was just noise. I agree with Jack. I likewise think that staring at a trading screen all day long is useless.

Markets move up and down, and when they move against you, when the screen is totally red, emotion can creep in, and we all know how detrimental that can be. I suggest that sometimes you simply switch off the screen and do something else. Pet the dog, make a sandwich, go to the gym, make another sandwich (there have been some years when I've gained 20 pounds!)—my point is to leave the scene and clear your head, then come back and decide what to do. You may be amazed at what you find when you return!

A TRADER'S WHOLE LIFE FITS IN A LITTLE BOX

Jack was a funny guy; he had very little in his office: a little box over in the corner, a few books on the desk, a light, and maybe one picture of his family—that was about it. He was a true minimalist. My office, in contrast, had tons of stuff in it: pictures, books, plaques, TV blaring, and so on. One day I went into Jack's office and I asked him, "Not for nothing, Jack, but what's the box for, and why don't you keep more stuff in your office?" He looked at me and said, "I can fit everything I have in this office in that little box in about two minutes." Jack's point was that he wanted to be ready to go at a moment's notice. After being a professional trader for a number of years, you come to learn that no matter where you're working as a trader it all comes down to results: You're only as good as your last trade.

Now, is that true? No, but it's the perception. Truthfully, the media can be an invaluable source of new information and also a good contraindicator. In other words, if everyone on TV or in the press is talking about how strong copper is, or crude oil, it may be time to look for a downside move—not always, but sometimes.

My advice is to use the news and information as a resource; pull out what you need and leave the rest behind. It's quite possible to be bombarded 24/7 by talking heads and then have no idea what to do. The best plan is to pick one or two trusted information sources, then lay out your own disciplined game plan and stick to it. Alter it occasionally, but never stray too far or too fast. You can always hit the mute button on the TV—sometimes that's your best move.

You'll preserve more of your sanity if you tune out all of the opinion and stick with the facts on which you should have based your trades in the first place. Moving your positions with every sound bite on TV makes only one person rich—your broker. Don't do it!

WHAT SOURCES OF INFORMATION DO INSIDERS FOLLOW?

In the world of commodities, figuring out which data *not* to look at can be just as important as knowing what you absolutely must follow on a regular basis. Each commodity is different, and learning what's important for corn is a lot different from learning what you need to watch for crude oil. Government numbers such as employment data, GDP, and Federal Reserve announcements impact almost all markets, even the global ones. It's important to have an understanding of the key reports and, even more essential, how much emphasis the markets place on them. Certain reports carry more weight with traders than others.

Furthermore, as a market changes and matures, certain reports may lose their relevance and new ones may come into play. For example, back when I started in the crude oil markets, everyone followed the American Petroleum Institute (API) report, the benchmark report for oil inventories. Not anymore. These days, traders monitor the Energy Information Agency (EIA) report.

Key government reports have been around for as long as the markets, and they rarely change. Unemployment numbers, trade deficit, GDP, consumer sentiment—all these are major indicators of the state of the economy, and traders should know when these numbers are going to be announced or published.

I've found that the hardest part about any information or number is not only understanding what it means but, more important, anticipating how the markets will react to the data. The second part of this equation is a thousand times more difficult than the first.

For example, if the EIA data for crude oil comes out on a Wednesday morning and it shows a build in crude oil supplies, will the market perceive that as bullish or bearish? In other words, if the report shows more crude oil on hand than expected, you would think that would tell traders the market is heading lower. Not always. Sometimes traders figure that OPEC will see that supply is higher and immediately cut production, which will have an impact on supplies down the road. So while the front couple of months may drop in price, if you own futures further out they actually could go higher. Commodities trading is like one big chess game; I advise being the knight, not a pawn. You always need to be flexible and agile when trading "off of the numbers." Remember not to get tunnel vision and don't fight the trend after a number—chances are very good that the trend will win.

"Buy the rumor, sell the news" is a common traders' saying, and for good reason. But once again this is not always the best advice. Sometimes the markets will already "price in" the anticipated data; then when the numbers are released it's a bit of a letdown from the hype before the number—thus, "Buy the rumor, sell the news." Another favorite old-time saying I used to hear is "Those who trade headlines end up selling newspapers."

Here are some of the key reports that professional traders follow:

- *Commitments of Traders (COT)*. A report published every Friday by the Commodity Futures Trading Commission (CFTC) that provides investors with up-to-date information on futures market operations and increases the transparency of the exchanges. This is one report that traders rely on heavily, and so should you.
- *Volume and open interest*. We talked about this. Open interest shows us how many people are actually trading any particular market at a given time. The higher the open interest, the safer, or at least more liquid, a market is to trade.
- *Commercials' positions*. This shows what commercial and end users are doing. Commercials buy more than individuals, or sell more, depending on market conditions. Traders put a lot of stock into what the commercials are doing because they carry a lot of weight in the market and often control the majority of the open interest.
- *Unemployment claims*. Jobs are the lifeblood of the economy, so traders pay very close attention to these numbers.

- *Interest rates.* Interest rates affect almost every aspect of people's lives, especially borrowing, and that can impact the ability of traders to invest, so it's important to keep an eye on the Federal Reserve at all times.

More specific to certain commodities are reports such as these:

- *Cattle on feed.* Shows the number of cattle that are in the process of getting ready for slaughter.
- *Crop Progress Report.* Shows the condition of the current crops and how and in what condition they may harvest.
- *Crop reports for orange juice.* Shows the orange crop estimates and potential damage from weather, pests, or disease.
- *EIA report for oil.* A weekly inventory report, appearing every Wednesday, for crude oil and products derived from it
- *Natural gas inventories.* Same as the EIA report for crude oil, except it comes out on Thursdays and measures only the amount of natural gas in storage in cubic feet.

. . . and many, many others.

Like any tool in our trading toolbox, these reports can help us make an educated trading decision, but remember that each is only one tool. Putting all of your eggs in one basket is never a good idea. Take the numbers with a grain of salt and try to anticipate how the market will react to any given number that is released. It's a good rule of thumb to be on the sidelines for any major announcement because trading ahead of a number is highly risky and often very unpredictable—but then again, that's what many investors want. As you gain experience, you'll be able to see where you want to be.

TRANSLATING AND DECIPHERING THE LANGUAGE OF THE MARKETS

If you've ever spent time in the visitor's gallery of a commodity futures exchange (and I encourage you to do so), you've heard the noise, seen the blur of the many different-colored jackets, and no doubt wondered what those seemingly random hand movements mean. To the normal outsider, the commodity futures markets definitely have a secret language, and a great part of that is hand signals. Hand signals—sometimes called the sign language of futures trading—are a unique way of conveying the basic information needed to conduct business on the trading floor. The signals let traders and other floor staff know how much of a commodity is being bid (the price that market participants are willing to pay for a commodity) and offered (the willingness to sell at a given price), how many contracts are at stake, what the expiration months are, the types of orders, and the status of the orders. Hand signals are the preferred form of floor communication for three main reasons:

1. *Speed and efficiency.* Hand signals enable fast communication over what can be long distances (as much as 30 or 40 yards) between the pits and order desks and within the pits themselves.
2. *Practicality.* Hands are more practical than voices because of the sheer number of people on the floor and the high noise level.
3. *Confidentiality.* Hand signals make it easier for customers to be anonymous, because large orders don't sit on a desk, where they can be seen by anyone and everyone.

Although they'd been around for decades, hand signals began to be used extensively in the early 1970s, when financial (rather than commodity-based) futures came on the scene. Although speed had long been a key element in futures trading, it became even more crucial when trading these instruments. Why? Because traders discovered they could take advantage of arbitrage opportunities between markets if they could trade quickly enough. (Simply put, arbitrage is the simultaneous purchase and sale of the same or an equivalent commodity or security to profit from price discrepancies. When price discrepancies emerge in the marketplace, the arbitrageur buys or sells until it's no longer profitable, or until prices are back in equilibrium.) Hand signals

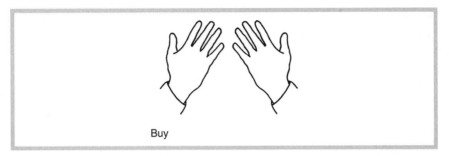

Figure 4.3 Buy.

met the need to speed up communication in the fast-moving financial futures pits.

Now, some examples.

Buy/Sell

When indicating you want an offer to buy (signaling a bid), the palm of the hand always faces toward you. You can remember this by thinking that when you're buying, you're pulling something in toward you. When making an offer to sell (offering), the palm always faces away from you. Think of selling as pushing something away from you. See Figures 4.3 and 4.4.

Price

To signal price, extend the hand in front of and away from the body. For the numbers one to five, hold your fingers straight up. For six

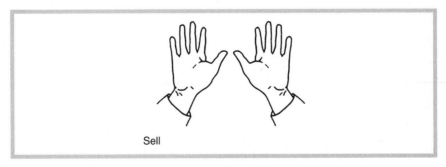

Figure 4.4 Sell.

through nine, hold them sideways. A clenched fist shows a zero, or "even."

Note: Price signals indicate only the last digit of a bid or offer. For example, a "0" (or even) signal might refer to a "40" bid. See Figure 4.5.

Quantity

To indicate quantity—the number of contracts being bid or offered—touch your face.

To signal quantities one through nine, touch your chin.

To show quantities in multiples of 10, touch your forehead.

To show quantities in multiples of 100, make a fist and touch your forehead. See Figure 4.6.

Knowing the Lingo

Ever take your car into the mechanic's shop and feel as if you were hearing a foreign language when they "explained" the problem(s) with your vehicle and what needed to be done to it? My mechanic's name is Vinny, and he sounds like a NASA scientist when he starts talking to me about my car. I simply end up nodding a lot, waiting to hear the final price for the repairs. I trust Vinny, but I'd still feel better if I knew at least the basics of what he was saying. Now, if you're like me, you put gas in your car, get it serviced regularly, make sure the spare is in the trunk, and then forget all about it. Until something goes wrong. Then you panic and you'll do (or pay) anything to fix it. The advantage is definitely with the mechanic. Don't get me wrong—I'm not saying that all mechanics are out to get you, but it sure helps you to deal with them when you know what they're talking about!

Well, in commodity trading, the advantage is definitely with those who know the lingo. You won't be able to make money if you don't know how to walk the walk and talk the talk.

Speculator? Scalper? Hedger? Contango (shall we dance?)? Backwardation? And on, and on, and on. . . . If you're totally confused, you're not alone. Don't be intimidated; at first I was, but that quickly faded. I remember when I first started my job at the exchange. Aside from the deafening noise levels and the frantic flailing of what seemed

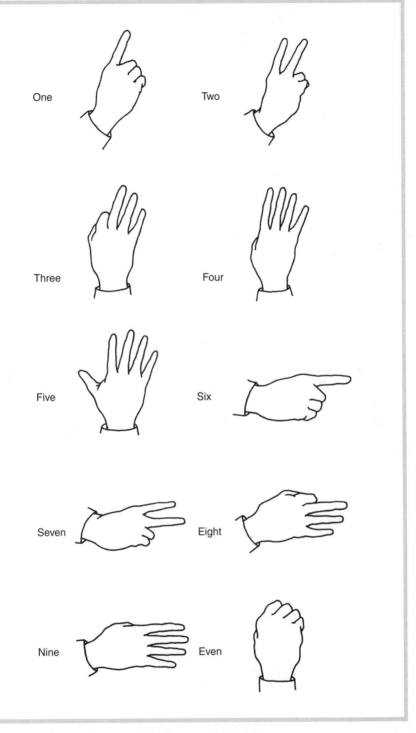

One   Two

Three   Four

Five   Six

Seven   Eight

Nine   Even

Figure 4.5 Prices.

Figure 4.6 Number of contracts to trade.

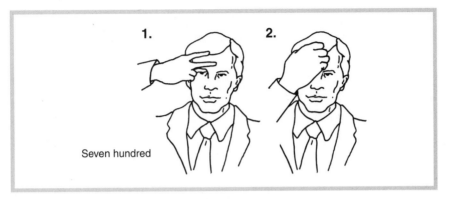

Figure 4.6 Number of contracts to trade, *continued.*

to be a bunch of crazies dressed in a montage of colored jackets, the language just boggled my mind. But once I learned a few key words and phrases and could tell a contingency order from a GTC, my comfort level rose considerably. And yours will, too. Trust me.

Who Are Those Guys?

First of all, you need to know the players. Basically, futures market participants are divided into two broad categories: *hedgers,* people who actually deal in the underlying commodity or financial instrument and seek insurance against adverse price fluctuations, and *speculators* (including professional floor traders like I used to be), who seek to profit from price swings. Speculators are often referred to as *locals.* Let's talk about the hedge side first.

The futures markets exist to facilitate risk management and are thus used extensively by hedgers—individuals or businesses that have exposure to the price of an agricultural commodity, or currency, or interest rates, for instance, and take futures positions designed to lessen their risks. This requires the hedger to take a futures position opposite that of his or her position in the actual cash commodity or financial instrument.

For example, sugar growers are at risk should the price of the commodity fall before they harvest and sell their crop. A short position in the futures market will return a profit when the price of sugar declines and the hedger's profit on the short futures position compensates for the loss on the physical commodity. Someone has to assume all this risk, and that's where you and I come in. Most likely, if you're like me, you're a speculator.

Speculators are attracted to futures trading purely and simply because they see the opportunity to profit from price swings in commodities and financial instruments. Speculators take advantage of the fact that the futures markets offer them access to price movements, the ability to offset their obligations prior to delivery, high leverage (low margin requirements), low transaction costs, and ease of assuming short as well as long positions (short futures positions, unlike short stock positions, are not subject to any sort of an uptick rule, nor to any broker/dealer interest charges).

In pursuit of trading profits, we speculators willingly take risks that hedgers wish to transfer. In this process, we provide the liquidity that ensures low transaction costs and reliable price discovery, those very market characteristics that make futures markets attractive to hedgers. So it's all really a big circle.

Both hedgers and speculators can be either bears or bulls, depending on the trend of the market. A market where prices are dropping is known as a *bear* market, and traders who expect a price decline are known as, not surprisingly, *bears*. On the opposite side is a *bull* market, one in which prices are rising. Those traders who act on that belief are called *bulls*. A good way to remember this is that a bear generally attacks by striking his paw downward, while a bull attacks by thrusting his horns upward. (Sources: Daniels Trading and Chicago Mercantile Exchange.)

Okay, those are the players. But what do they do?

Order Types

These are some of the most common questions I am asked: How do I place an order to buy or sell in commodities markets? What are the choices? There are many types of orders when placing commodities trades: limit orders, market orders, sell orders, buy orders, and contingency orders. A contingency order is, literally, contingent on something else. For example, O.C.O. stands for "one cancels other." In other words, this order is saying that if one order is filled, it cancels another. The following are some other common contingency orders:

- *Market order (MKT).* Used to get into or out of a market either long or short at whatever the market is trading at right now. It's the fastest and easiest type for a floor broker (the trader in the pits) to fill. This trade should be filled within three minutes or less. This order is time-sensitive, not price-sensitive.
- *Stop order (STP).* This order is price-sensitive. A stop order becomes a market order only if the commodity you are trading hits a certain price or trades through it. This trade should be filled within five minutes or less by the floor broker. This time-sensitive trade has some price sensitivity, but if the markets are moving quickly, your fill price may slip some from where you originally placed it. Slippage is not uncommon. This order is used for stop losses (more about those later).
- *Limit order (LMT/OB).* You would use this order when you are looking to buy a certain commodity at a certain price or less than what the market is trading at, or sell a certain commodity at any price above where the market is currently. Always remember that this is a price-sensitive order only and is a lower priority than the market stop order.
- *Or better order (OB).* A type of a limit order in which the market is at or better than the limit specified. The term is often used to help clarify that the order was not mistakenly given as a limit when it looks like it should be a stop order.
- *Market if touched (MIT).* This order is similar to the limit order in many respects, except for one key thing. If you're trying to sell your commodity for a certain price and the market goes up and touches that price, your order is filled at the market. This does not mean that your order will be filled at the price you wanted, but it does mean that it must be filled within five minutes from when the market first hit your price. If you've ever wondered why everyone seems so frantic in the trading pit, this is why.

And here are some other terms you might find handy:

- *Day traders.* Speculators who take positions in commodity futures or options contracts and liquidate them before the end of the trading day.
- *Scalp.* To trade for small gains. Scalping normally involves establishing and liquidating a position quickly, usually within the same day, hour, or even just a few minutes.
- *Spreading.* The simultaneous buying and selling of two related markets in the expectation that a profit will be made when the position is offset. Examples include buying one futures contract and selling another futures contract of the same commodity but different delivery month; buying and selling the same delivery month of the same commodity on different futures exchanges; buying a given delivery month of one futures market and selling the same delivery month of a different, but related, futures market.

The Changing Language of the Markets

Like anything else, the language of the commodity markets has evolved over time, and with the addition of new contracts and the advent of electronic trading. So just when you think you've learned it all, some new commodity you never even thought of trading enters the picture and, with it, a whole new vocabulary to learn. The energy marketsare a good example.

These markets employ a number of terms that seem strange, if not downright bizarre, such as *sweet* and *sour.* No, not pork, crude oil. Crude oil is not on your local Chinese restaurant menu, but it does come in sweet and sour varieties. Sweet crude simply means it has less sulfur content than sour crude, which thus has more sulfur content. Refiners prefer the light sweet crude because it's easier and cleaner to refine and produces less residual waste and damage to their machinery.

Here are two more good ones: *backwardation* and *contango.* Each explains a price and supply condition. Backwardation is a market condition in which spot prices exceed forward prices. Contango is not a dance—it's when forward prices exceed spot prices. These terms are most commonly used in the energy markets but are applied in other commodities and markets, too.

By now that auto mechanic sounds like a paragon of simplicity. But this is only the tip of the terminology iceberg. You'll find much more in the glossary at the end of this book.

As you go along, when you come across any terminology that you're not sure of, always ask your broker or look it up online. There are numerous resources on the Web; don't be afraid to use them.

CONCLUSION

Now that you've had a glimpse of the inner workings and psychology of the commodity trading world, you're either chomping at the bit to find out more or in a state of total panic. Trust me, it gets better. I'm not here to scare you but to make you want to participate in these markets and not feel intimidated by them. The more you learn, the more comfortable you'll be, and the more eager to join this club and make some significant money. So read on!

CHAPTER 5

DIGGING DEEPER

WHAT THE TRADERS IN THE PIT NEVER REVEAL

THE THINGS THE FLOOR DOESN'T NECESSARILY WANT
YOU TO KNOW

You recognize some of the jargon, you've learned some of the psychology, and you know some of the questions to ask. But that's just the tip of the commodity trading iceberg. There are so many things a trader new to commodities should know. Some are easy to find out; some aren't. Seasoned commodities traders with consistently successful track records know all of these things and have almost always learned them either from a more experienced trader or, unfortunately, by trial and error. I prefer the first way, and I think you will, too.

While it would be impossible to cover all of the aspects of trading in this book, the following are what I think are a good starting point for novices. For those more experienced traders, the information that follows will help you take your trading to the next level.

Order, Order!

Every trader has a toolbox, but not every trader uses it. Deciding which tools to use, and when, is vital to being a profitable trader. Some of the most important tools in the toolbox are order types. We talked about some of these in Chapter 4, but now it's time to see how they're used. While there are many types of orders, I'm going to concentrate on what I think of as the primary four; these are also the ones I use the most, as most traders do.

I know countless stories, including a few based on my own experience, about people who had a GTC order working and called their broker, deciding to get out of the market. What happens? Usually the person forgets to cancel the GTC order or the broker doesn't catch it,

---

MARKET ORDER (MKT)

Buy 1 October Live Cattle (LCV7) at the Market

"If a market is worth trading, it's worth trading with a market order." A woman I knew on the trading desk used to say this, and it can be very true indeed, but with some caveats.

A *market order* typically is used to get into or out of a market, either long or short, at whatever the market is trading at right now. It's the fastest and easiest type for a floor broker to fill. A market order in a very liquid market will often be the best way to go if you know where the market is in advance. But in a very *illiquid* market, these orders can be devastating. Brokers rarely will "work" a market order; after all, it's their job to fill a market order within a set amount of time, usually only a few minutes. If they don't, they can owe you a fill at a better price—something they don't want to do because it costs them money. So market orders should be used when you absolutely want to be in or out of a position, and only when you have a fair idea of where you can actually get filled.

Not using a market order can be frustrating because you won't always get into the trade you want. So using or not using a market order is something that needs to be taken on a case-by-case basis with every trade. Even seasoned traders grapple with this decision, so don't feel alone. For example, sometimes I want to get into a market so badly I'm willing to use a market order, and I always end up paying too much for the trade even if I eventually make a profit; this is a bad habit to get into. Use market orders only when absolutely needed; otherwise, use a limit order.

LIMIT ORDER (LMT/OB)

Maniac Futures
Buy 1 October Live Cattle (LCV7) at 90.32 Limit

The *limit order* is pretty much the opposite of a market order. You would use this order if you wanted to buy a certain commodity at a certain price or at less than what the market is trading at, or sell a certain commodity at any price above where the market is currently. Always remember, this is a price-sensitive order *only* and is of a lower priority than the market stop order.

When a market order isn't the best choice, as already explained, a trader probably would use a limit order. Limit orders indicate an exact price at which you want to either enter or exit a trade; they can't be filled at any worse than the price on the order, but *can* be filled at a better price, if possible. In other words, if you wanted to buy November gold at $625 and gold is currently trading at $626, then the broker would be unable to buy you the gold contract until it comes down to your price. However, let's say you put in an order to buy gold at $625 and the market opens at $624; then the broker might be able to buy the gold for you at that much better price. It works the same way for a sell order.

Limit orders are one of the best ways to go for most trading because they help you set specific measurable goals for your trading and also ensure a level of discipline. Not chasing the market is a good habit to have, and using limit orders is a great way to learn that discipline.

There are many different types of limit orders, and by working with your broker it's easy to figure out different strategies for using all of them when appropriate. Often, getting into a trade is only half the challenge; the harder part for many traders can be getting out of a trade with or without profits. That's where stop orders come in.

which is not necessarily his or her job anyway. Next thing you know, the trade this person thought was closed is suddenly reopened! Let me clarify. A GTC order will continue to be in place no matter what you do, unless you specifically cancel it, with either your broker or your online electronic trading platform. Considering the rapid pace of the market, it can be easy to forget the orders that you have working. But

STOP ORDER (STP)

Maniac Futures
Sell 1 October Live Cattle (LCV7) at 90.21 Stop

Stop orders are as important to a trader as water is to a fish. Stop orders safeguard profits, they protect against staggering losses, and they help a trader to initiate a new position at a specific level. Stop orders also are called *stop-loss* orders. They don't, of course, stop losses; they just help to limit them.

A stop order becomes a market order only if the commodity you're trading hits a certain price or trades through it. This time-sensitive trade has some price sensitivity, but if the markets are moving quickly, it's not unusual for your fill price to slip some from where you originally placed it.

When you have a position—let's say, our long gold position from $625—you're hoping the price goes higher so that you can sell the contract at a profit. However, if the gold decides instead to back off to, say, $623, you want to have a stop order in place to protect yourself against a major loss. We would place a sell stop at $623. A sell stop always goes below the market, and a buy stop always goes above, for obvious reasons.

Stop orders can be tricky. Set a stop too close and it will get *elected* (traded or filled) quickly. Set a stop too far away and it doesn't really serve its purpose. Learning to use stops effectively takes time and effort but can be well worth it.

Stop orders also are sometimes used to initiate a position once a certain price level is reached, and only then. In other words, if you want to enter gold at $625 as a seller and the market is at $626, you want to wait for the market to begin to drop again before selling, so you would use a $625 stop to enter.

There are other types of stop orders—stop limits, for example—and those are strategies that are best discussed with your broker before each trade. Sometimes limit orders are not filled immediately; that's when patience is definitely a virtue. Stop orders are used in futures trading and not in options—at least not normally—and most options markets wouldn't accept them. However, a trader can always use a mental stop to set a level at which to get out.

Orders are almost always considered good for the day unless otherwise specified. That's when a good till canceled order comes into play.

GOOD TILL CANCELED (GTC)

Maniac Futures
Buy 1 October Live Cattle (LCV7) at 90.32
or Better GTC (Good Till Canceled)

As I've said, typically an order is good for the day—a *day order*—but sometimes the day's trading action doesn't fill your order, and you have to wait. You would enter a *good till canceled* (GTC) order. Also known as an *open order*, a GTC order is in effect until it's canceled, filled, or the contract expires.

These orders are considered contingency orders, which are any type of order with special instructions. A contingency order is contingent on something else. In this case your order is good until you cancel it. Be careful to specify that you want your order to be a GTC, because brokers and online trading systems are not mind readers and won't assume it to be a GTC. More than likely, they'll place it as a day order unless you specifically indicate that the order is "GTC" or "open order." If you're not sure they understood you, ask your broker to read the order back to you and always get an order number. An order number for your GTC or even a day order helps you keep good records, and helps your broker, too.

An order number can be vital in case you forget about a GTC order. Always be sure to keep track of your GTC orders—don't forget about them. This is a common mistake and can cost you money.

it's just as easy to avoid these nasty surprises. Simply write down your orders and check them with your broker each day. Using a limit order with a GTC is usually the best way to enter or exit the market, unless conditions indicate otherwise.

To Spread or Not to Spread: That's Some Question

Now that you have a good handle on the basic order types, let's tackle another, more complex, order type. Next to options trading, spread trading confuses more new traders than any other type of trading order.

It's actually quite simple if you don't let all the jargon make you nervous. Basically, you're taking simultaneous long and short positions in an attempt to profit. The profit comes from the differential, or *spread,* between two prices. A spread can be established between different months of the same commodity (called an *interdelivery spread*); between the same or related commodities, usually for the same month (*intercommodity spread*); or between the same or related commodities traded on two different exchanges (*intermarket spread*).

You can enter a spread order at the market, or you can designate that you want to be filled when the price difference between the commodities reaches a certain point (or premium). Take this spread example: We want to buy 1 June Live Cattle and Sell 1 August Live Cattle when the August cattle contract is 100 points higher than the June contract. The order would read something like this:

Buy 1 June Live Cattle, Sell 1 August Live Cattle plus 100 to the August Sell Side

Sounds confusing, but, trust me, it's not. Again, all this means is that you want to initiate or liquidate the spread when the August cattle contract price is 100 points higher than that of the June cattle. These days, most exchanges don't report spread transactions on their quote boards, but a few do. The best method is to find out from your broker, who will call the trading floor or the order desk and ask them to get a "fresh quote." Another way to figure out where a spread might be is to take the two prices and simply add or subtract one from the other. Always confirm this with your broker or the trading floor before entering any spread trade.

Like everything in commodities, once you get used to the basics of trading spreads, you'll become aware of more complex strategies that include but are not limited to condor spreads, crack spreads, and crush spreads—the list goes on ad infinitum. No, a condor isn't an exotic bird of prey; it's simply trading-ese for a rather exotic spread trade. Condor spreads are sometimes referred to as "elongated butterflies." That helps a lot, right? Let's try another approach.

Take a long call condor spread: This bird consists of a long call of a lower strike, one short call of a second strike, one short call of a third strike, and, finally, a long call of a fourth strike. The calls have the same expiration, and the strikes are an equal distance apart. Now, you're probably scratching your head and saying, "When would I ever use this?" Exactly! A condor spread is such a specialized strategy that it's hard to say what the individual's reasoning would be for using it; it would be different on a case-by-case basis.

I will say that spread trading—even complicated spreads like condors—can have value for some investors. I'm in no way advocating this type of trading, even for a seasoned options trader like myself. The biggest and most glaring problem with these complex spreads is that the only person who usually makes money is your broker. Condor spreads, like butterfly spreads, involve significant transaction costs, which make them prohibitive for option traders who do not qualify for major commission discounts. The cost of this position must be examined carefully before establishing it.

The best thing to do is avoid trading any of these complex option strategies altogether. The risks of these option spreads far outweigh the advantages, and sometimes they are far more hassle then they could ever be worth.

Some other types of spreads are more mainstream and do offer good opportunity. Two of those involve a main commodity that has products created or derived from it. A crush spread, for example, is simply a spread between soybeans and soybean meal and or soybean oil, sometimes called *putting on the crush*. A crack spread has nothing to do with illegal drugs; it's the same type of spread as the crush, only it involves crude oil and unleaded gasoline and/or heating oil.

Let me interrupt myself for a second—I know all of this lingo can sound like mumbo jumbo, but rest assured that as you need to know these things, you will. When I was first introduced to the markets, I felt completely lost. I was utterly bombarded with a whole spectrum of new expressions and terms my first few weeks on the trading floor. Although the old saying "Fake it till you make it" worked for me, I suggest instead finding a broker or trading mentor, much as my readers have found in me. Use this person, ask questions, solicit advice, and whenever you're not sure of what the terminology means, ask.

In my experience, people usually like nothing better than to talk about themselves; they like to teach someone something they know.

So never hesitate to ask the questions; after all, it's the only way you'll learn.

Spreads can be valuable and profitable, but it's important to start with the basics and then move on to the more exotic stuff when and if appropriate. Whenever I have an important decision to make, I compile two lists: pro versus con. Here are some basic pros and cons of spread trading.

Pros

- Spreads in commodity futures offer lower margin rates because these strategies usually carry less risk. (We'll talk more about margins in a minute.)
- Spreads are usually less volatile and prices move less quickly, which can be good for beginners who may be intimidated by the speed and price fluctuations of a single outright trade in the futures market.
- Spreads offer unique hedging opportunities in a variety of commodities.
- Certain types of spread trading allow the trader to pay less in margin, funding the purchased future or option with the sale of the other side of the spread, thus reducing initial costs.

Cons

- Spread trading has much higher transaction (commission) costs because you're using more than one trading vehicle. That's why it's even more important for a spread trader to have an excellent entry and exit point, because every penny will count.
- Spreads are often not traded outright—in other words. on their own—in some commodities, so you must "leg" into them which can be tricky for the novice (more about outrights versus legging into trades in the section on locals later in this chapter).
- Spreads can be less liquid than other trades, which could prove to be disastrous if you're trying to get out of a position in a hurry.
- Spreads have limited profit potential most of the time. For example, if a trader buys July corn and sells December and the July rallies but the December contract doesn't really fall by much and,

in fact, rallies, too, then the trader's profits would be limited and the extra commissions would cut into what little profit the trader made.

• Spread trading can be confusing, especially to the newer trader.

My final word on spread trading: It can be effective, but before entering into any spread trade, figure out if you really have a reason to be using this type of trade—what purpose does it serve? If the answer is clear to you, then go right ahead. Remember, the most important thing to watch with spreads are those pesky transaction costs—they can really add up fast.

Options: Overcoming the Fear Factor and Zeroing In on Profits

Early in my career there was one area of trading that I avoided like the plague: options—or options on futures, to be precise. I thought they were too complicated, too expensive, too risky. It took me a long time to learn that all my fears were misguided. In fact, options have ended up being the most profitable part of my trading by far.

Now, I was no math maven in school. I've struggled since Mr. Richardson's sixth-grade math tests, especially the five-minute one. (I still wake up in a cold sweat over that one.) Let me tell you, his math tests kept me after school many a day and destroyed any interest in math that I might ever have had. All through the rest of my academic life I always did exceptionally well in vocabulary, reading, and writing, but stunk at math in all forms except geometry, which my brain confused with drawing. Still, to this day, I'm a terrible mathematician and rely on all the modern-day conveniences, such as accountants.

Nevertheless, if, like me, you spent a lot of time after school for math, then you, too, may think you're not able to trade options. Think again.

Some options books can be mind-boggling, with complicated mathematical equations and lots of detailed explanations that would mystify even Einstein, all to try and explain a simple concept.

Because this is not strictly an options book, we won't go into great detail here; there are plenty of resources for that on the Internet or in

---

OPTIONS ON FUTURES

Each option specifies:
- The right to buy or sell a futures contract (the underlying)
- The commodity

---

your local bookstore. All you need to do is understand the basics of options and how they can immediately benefit your portfolio in ways you couldn't imagine. Right about now you're probably saying, "Okay, how?"

- Options limit risk and give you unlimited profits.
- Options give you tons of leverage in an already highly leveraged market.
- Options can allow you to trade markets you may not otherwise be able to afford to trade due to extremely high margins (e.g., natural gas, gold, crude oil).
- Options limit risk and give you unlimited profits. It's worth repeating this one: *Options limit risk and give you unlimited profits.*

Options ABCs

Before you do anything, you simply must learn the basics of options, there are no two ways about that—even the Maniac Trader had to succumb at some point! Forget your fear—if this sixth-grade math dropout can do it and be consistently successful, so can you.

So let's begin. A *call* option is what we buy when we think the market is going higher; a *put* option is what we buy when we think the market is headed lower. Either way, the goal is the same: to make money from the difference between the strike price of the option and

---

SOME BASIC OPTIONS TERMS

Call option: The right to buy a futures contract at a specific price
Put option: The right to sell a futures contract at a

the current market rate of the investment. For purposes of this book we'll only discuss buying options. Buying options, either puts or calls, involves limited risk and unlimited profit potential. You can sell options (also called *writing* options), but this carries with it limited profit potential and unlimited risk. Selling or shorting options is highly risky; if you're new to trading and even if you're not, many brokerage firms won't let you do it. So let's just focus on buying calls and puts.

When we buy a call or put we have to pay what is called *premium*. *Premium* is a fancy way of saying what you're going to have to fork over for the option position. You can calculate what a fair premium should be in many ways, but at first it's best to work with a broker who has experience in calculating a fair value for the option; get the broker to help you learn how to do it, and don't take no for an answer. (We'll learn more about fair value in Chapter 6.)

Most of the time you can find out where the option that you want to buy is trading the same way you get futures quotes—in the newspaper or on the Internet. If not, your broker can call the floor and get a fresh quote, much as the broker might do with spread orders. It's a good idea anyway because sometimes there are so many options they don't all get updated and the price information on the screen may not be the most current. Always check first before trading.

Now I've gotten ahead of myself a bit. Why exactly am I buying an option in the first place? Why not just buy a cattle futures contract if I think it's going higher? Great question. Answer: two *big* advantages.

The first huge advantage is that when you buy options you're not required to put up any margin. Nope . . . zip, zero, nada. In other words, for something like cattle futures you would need to put up around $945 per contract as a guarantee or margin, and that money would remain locked up for the length of the trade. If you were to buy a cattle option instead, you would not have to post the margin at all and could use that $945 toward other trades or simply keep it liquid. This is one of the greatest attractions of trading options: not tying up capital with margins.

Second, options allow you to control a vast amount of a particular commodity at a ridiculously low price. Leverage again—we love leverage! As you know, futures allow you to do this, but to a much lesser extent. Also, futures carry unlimited risk, as I pointed out earlier, while the risk in options is limited to just the premium you pay, nothing more. Now, the trick is finding bargains in options and knowing what the risk/reward potential is. This is where many traders come unstuck.

Major Options Dos and Don'ts: The Maniac Trader's
Pet Peeves

There are plenty of blunders people can make when it comes to options, but a few really stand out and I'll share them with you now.

- *Chasing the market doesn't pay.* Never, never, never do this. This holds true even more for options than for futures. Chasing after a trade in a market means you'll end up paying too much or selling for too little. In options trading this can mean the difference between consistently making and losing money. Remember, options have an intrinsic value when you purchase them, and the time value is always whittling away. The option is constantly depreciating, like some new car from hell. So, no matter what it takes, avoid overpaying for an option—it will be even harder to turn a profit when it comes time to close the position.
- *Time is on your side.* Don't buy options with too little time value. Time value is one of the most important things in options, and for that asset you have to pay more premium, but it can be worth it. The more time you have on your side, the more chance your trade has of making money. Buy too close in, say, one or two months, and you may not have enough time until expiration for any real price movement. I don't advise trading options with less than 3 months until expiration or more than 18 months.
- *"Cheap" doesn't always mean good.* Stay away from way out-of-the-money strike prices. Way, way out-of-the-money strike prices for commodities may be cheaper, but the old saying "You get what you pay for" usually applies. If the option is so far out of the money—say, in heating oil—that it will take an ice age to get to that price level, then "cheap" is a relative term. Try to buy

a strike price that's only slightly out of the money unless you feel very strongly that the market is going to make a significant move in your favor; then you want to buy deep, way out-of-the-money options, as they're called.

As important as knowing what not to do is learning what you should do to get a decent entry point for an option.

Bargain Hunting

Options trading can be like heading to the store for that big sale and finding your most desired item at half off, which somehow makes it an even more valuable treasure. Nothing feels better than a bargain, no matter what it is. First things first, however: You must know fair value for the option to determine whether the premium is a bargain.

So do that first, then begin to price out different options that have at least 3 months, but no more than 18 months, until expiration. There are always exceptions, but those are two of my general rules. Once you've picked the option month you want to trade, see where the underlying futures are and make a note of it.

Remember, a critical element of options is time value, also called *time decay* (the other element is intrinsic value—more about that later). An option is often referred to as a wasting asset, mainly because time erodes some of the option each day as it gets nearer to expiration. This is why it's vital to give the option enough time to mature and grow. In my opinion, less than three months is simply not enough time value.

What Price Options?

So you've chosen the month and length of your option, and the commodity itself, of course; now you can begin to bargain-hunt. Strike prices are the different prices at which you can trade options; each commodity has different strike prices and rules, so you have to look at each one individually.

Strike prices can be out of the money, in the money, or at the money. For example, if you buy a call option with a strike price that's below the current futures price, it would be in the money; if the strike price is exactly the same as the futures price at the moment, it's considered to be at the money; and if the option is above the current trading price, it's out of the money. Of course, the opposite applies for a put option.

So you'll need to decide if you want to buy in-the-money or out-of-the-money options. For obvious reasons, in-the-money options usually require much greater premium because they have more intrinsic value in those options. (Here we go again: *Intrinsic value* is the positive difference between the current price for the underlying futures contract and the strike price of the option. For a call option, the strike price has to be *under* the futures price; for a put option, the strike price has to be *over* the futures price.) Out-of-the-money options require less and less premium the further out you go.

Which option to choose must be decided on a case-by-case basis for each trade. but once again the most important thing is to know to the best of your ability what a good basis is for fair value for the option—this can spare you a lot of headaches later.

So there you have a very broad overview of options. In Chapter 6 we'll talk about more rules for effectively trading options and why most people fail at it. But now let's take a closer look at margin calls and how to avoid them as much as possible when trading futures.

When Margin Calls

Margins can be confusing for new traders, so let me see if I can make it simple, because it really is. *Margin* is simply what you need, money-wise, to trade futures. The clearinghouse your broker works for is essentially like a bank, and this "bank" is only interested in protecting its assets; whether you make or lose money is more or less irrelevant to them, although they may never say that to you. Margin also is called a *performance bond* or a *guarantee* or something similar.

All margin does is provide integrity and security in the market—if functions as a kind of insurance policy. Trading commodities can be volatile and fast-paced, so everyone needs to know that everyone else has the funding to ensure the market will function and everyone can meet their obligations. Loss of confidence in a market's ability to meet the transactions could be devastating, so to prevent this, the exchanges set what is called *exchange minimums* for margin. This is the minimum an individual needs in his or her account to trade a commodity. Brokerage firms can charge even more if they choose (most do), to avoid risk at all costs. Some markets are more margin-intensive than others because they're more volatile. For example, natural gas is a highly volatile market and has one of the highest margins around—$18,000 per contract—while corn is one of the lowest at $450. Of course, these change as market conditions change and can increase or decrease depending on liquidity and market action.

Initial and Maintenance Margin

Initial margin is what you must have in your account to initiate a position. *Maintenance margin* is an amount that must be maintained on deposit in your margin account at all times. If the equity in the account drops to or below this level because prices move against you, the broker would issue a margin call to restore your equity to the initial level. Let's take a simple example.

To trade corn, you would need at least $450 per contract (or whatever current margin is) as required by your brokerage firm and the exchange, plus additional funds to handle any fluctuation in daily trading. Now let me explain. Say we have $1,000 in our account and we want to buy 1 July corn future. First of all, we would need $450 for the initial margin. Then if we were long the corn and it went down, money would be debited from the remaining $550 in our account.

If things went sharply against us and corn fell off a cliff and the loss went beyond $550, we would now be dipping into that margin we had put up initially, depleting the account. That's when we'd get a margin call. Margin calls are usually brought to your attention long before you get close to them, and you usually will be given the option of adding more funds to your account immediately or selling the position in the account at a loss. If you don't take action either way, it will be taken for you by our friend the margin clerk.

Some ways to avoid margin calls are to keep your account well funded, avoid trading high-margin futures, and to avoid margin altogether, simply buy options, which require no margin. In options, the premium is all you pay; it's also all you can lose, so margin isn't necessary.

Margin actually is a good thing. It adds security and integrity to the market and ensures that each transaction is backed by the full faith of the clearinghouse and exchange. Margin is what allows traders to have such high leverage and control an incredible amount of any given commodity for only pennies on the dollar. But it has its dark side—it also can allow you to overextend before you know it, and this can be a very fast way to end up broke. So don't do it.

Important note to equity traders: Buying on margin in stocks is different from buying on margin in futures; in stocks, margin is a down payment, whereas in futures, it's a performance bond. This is a very big difference. Also, selling a futures contract doesn't require additional margin or specialized permission for your account. However, selling options on their own (also called *writing naked options*) is highly risky and requires authorization as well as heavy margin.

There's a lot of information about margin available from the various exchanges and certainly from your brokerage firm. Learn all you can.

Let the Locals Work for You

What is a local? Well, let me give you just a few words about the trading pit and the environs of the floor. A *local* is a member of the exchange who simply trades for his or her personal account. Locals usually *scalp* to make money. That's why they're sometimes called *scalpers.* They shave off a point here or there on trades that come into the pit, buying at a fraction below the last transaction price and selling at a fraction above; they buy and sell rapidly, with small profits or losses, and hold their positions for as little as a few minutes during the trading session.

At the end of the day they hope to have made money; sometimes they do and sometimes they don't. Locals serve an important purpose in any market: They provide liquidity and integrity in the price discovery process. In other words, they help keep prices fair. When they see that a price is out of whack, they will jump in and *make a market,* hoping to make money on the discrepancy.

I mentioned earlier, when we talked about spreads, that locals—and all floor traders, for that matter—actually have the ability to leg into spreads. This is a distinct advantage. Why, and what is legging? *Legging* means that you can trade one side of the spread at a time. (This is unlike traders off the floor, who tend to buy the spreads outright when they're offered that way.) Like scalping, this ability to leg is easier to do on the floor. Traders off the floor can do it, too; it's just more difficult to execute.

When you're trading you need to keep in mind that the locals are making a market. They'll likely help you avoid chasing the market as much if you let them do their job, so be patient, set your price, and let the market come to you. Locals are a dying breed in a way because as more and more markets go electronic it's tougher and tougher for the locals to make their living; electronic markets have made trading even more transparent and have limited scalping opportunities. It's becoming harder to scalp and take advantage of trading in the pit.

Now when your broker tells you the floor is saying that the locals are buying or selling, you'll know what he or she is talking about.

FINE-TUNING YOUR TRADING ACTION PLAN

I've told you how vital it is for a new trader to ask questions, and then more questions. One thing that really can be helpful for you, too, is to visit one of the exchanges in Chicago or New York. Since 9/11, it can be more difficult because of much tighter security, but if it's at all possible for you, it can give you a really good feel for what actually goes on and what it looks, sounds, and smells like.

Another place to visit is your broker's office. Ask if you can meet the staff in person. When you go in for the appointment, try to meet the branch manager, the margin clerk, and the back-office people. Also, you'll want to know your broker's backup person. Brokers get sick and take vacations like the rest of us, and usually they have someone cover for them. It's a good idea to know who these people are ahead of time so you're not a stranger when the time comes that you need to deal with them.

Let me share a good example with you. Early in my career, the top broker at the firm I was with had gone on vacation and his biggest client (whom he didn't let anyone else even talk to) was a major trader. He had about a $20 million account and would throw around 100-lots in Standard & Poor's (the S&P) like most people throw around 1 contract in corn; in other words, he was big, very BIG. Well, the senior broker had arranged to have one specific broker whom he trusted handle this man's account. The broker he picked to cover him while he was away had an emergency appendectomy and was out when the big trader called in. The brokers were not aware of all of his working orders and accounts; they missed a GTC order the man wanted to cancel, and it was filled—*yikes!*

It was a 100-lot order in crude oil, and ended up costing around $35,000. It was a mess. The lesson is this: Have your broker introduce you to his or her trading partner. Many brokers work as teams. Also, and more important, don't ever rely too heavily on your broker.

I keep copies of all of my trades and order tickets, and so should you. Get in the habit of writing out a little order ticket each time you place a new order with your broker. When the broker tells you the order number, write it down; if they don't give you one (which they will if you ask), then make one up and give it to them, just so you have a record to track the order. It is critical that you keep track of GTC orders, or this same scenario could happen to you.

At the start and end of each trading day, just ask your broker to check your open orders (GTCs). Here's what I typically say to my broker in the morning, followed by an afternoon version; each conversation lasts all of about three minutes.

> Good morning, Charlie, I need to check my open orders. I'm working to sell 2 December corn at 268 GTC order number 456; I'm working to buy 1 July cocoa on a 56 stop GTC order 388, and to sell 1 August unleaded 218 GTC ticket number 343. Is that all you have?

Then at the end of the trading day we would do a checkout of the day's activity and at that time also recheck all of the open orders.

Hey good afternoon, Charlie. I just want to check out, okay? We sold 1 August unleaded 18 on ticket number 343—my open order, right? Good fill. So now I'm simply working my two other GTC orders—ticket 456 to sell 2 December corn at 268 and order number 388 to buy 1 July cocoa on a 56 stop, GTC. Is that correct?

Checking in and checking out are things all good brokers do for their own protection and yours. Never feel bad about asking them to do it—they'll appreciate the fact that you're proactive and are keeping track of your orders. Right after the close of the markets, the brokers can be frantically busy, so always give them a few minutes to get their order tickets organized before you call them to check out. Now, once the trades for a certain day have been checked with you, it's up to the back-office people to get them all into the right account.

The folks in the back office are the ones who put together your daily trading statements and also handle check requests, out trades (trades that don't match up), and many other things—in other words, all the nitty-gritty that keeps the firm running. It never hurts to be on a first-name basis with someone in the back office. All this is food for thought for a new trader—this info can be vital at certain times.

THE MANIAC TRADER'S TOP FIVE WAYS TO BECOME YOUR BROKER'S FAVORITE CLIENT WITHOUT PAYING THE MOST COMMISSIONS

1. *Commission myths: You get what you pay for.* Yes, usually. There's nothing wrong with wanting to save money on commissions, but sometimes paying a little more can mean the difference between making money and losing your shirt. I've been in this business for almost two decades, yet I have a full-service broker I can call at any time. Why? Because sometimes even the Maniac Trader needs help! I may need my broker to execute a special offset (more about that later), I may want a second opinion, I may be having problems entering an order online,

and so on. If I'm paying the lowest rate going, I may not be able to get anyone on the phone, and by the time I do, the market could have moved against me and cost me far more than the little extra commission I would have paid.

2. *Quid pro quo: Ask for a better commission rate.* It's okay to ask for a better (read: lower) commission rate, but an alternative is to find out exactly what you're getting for that higher commission. Maybe the brokerage is offering free or discounted future quotes, news services, or other services. If you don't ask for stuff, it's unlikely they'll offer, so ask.

3. *Great expectations: Brokers have little if any control over margins, so don't bother.* Establish expectations right up front and don't call your broker every two minutes, but tell them ahead of time how often you'll need to talk to them or will need to hear from them. If you have special needs, let them know—that's what they're there for and if they can't do it, it's their responsibility to tell you so.

4. *Quality counts: Good brokers share certain traits.* The top qualities of the best brokers include patience, understanding, and a willingness to teach. A good broker should not have too many clients and will know you by name (bonus: also knowing your kids' names). The broker should be reputable, having no problems with the NFA or customer complaints on record. Seek a broker with at least 10 years' experience (bonus: a broker who has worked on the trading floor). Finally, the best brokers will exhibit honesty, integrity, and concern for your long-term success.

5. *Worth the price: Why self-directed accounts can end up costing you more.* As I mentioned earlier, cutting costs on commissions can come back to bite you, big-time. Let me share a glaring example of a new trader who wrote to me a year or so ago. He was an experienced equity trader but a complete novice in the futures arena. He was used to paying a small, $7 commission for virtually unlimited shares and was appalled at the idea of paying $50 for only one futures contact ($25 per side). This trader opened an online account for $12 a trade and bought

10 S&P 500 contracts at $250 per point. Unfortunately, the market began to go against him, and in a panic he *bought* another 10 S&P contracts online, using the automated trading platform, when he thought he had *sold* them to cover the position. He didn't realize the mistake until a few hours later, when the market was closed. The next day the market was even lower, and now he was long 20, not 10! The entire trade was liquidated, costing him around $18,000. A full-service broker never would have allowed this to happen. So while he saved some money initially, it ended up costing a lot more in the end. Just keep it in mind.

SUMMARY AND CONCLUSION

By now, things should be coming together for you. You recognize some of the lingo, you know some of the players, you've heard what kind of questions to ask, and we're beginning to dig beneath the surface of that commodity trading iceberg.

Let's review what we've discussed in this chapter:

- Use that toolbox! Deciding which tools to use, and when, is one of the most important things you can learn.
- Find a well-seasoned broker or trading mentor, and use this person. Most people like to help and will be happy to answer your questions. Just ask.
- Use spread trading judiciously. Remember, those transaction costs can add up before you know it.
- Don't be afraid of options—little outlay, lots of profit potential.
- Make sure you know what you're getting for your commission fees—keep in mind that saving on commissions can be a double-edged sword.
- Margin—good news and bad news. It gives security and integrity to the market and allows you to control a lot of commodity for a little money. But beware of that false sense of security—don't become overextended.

It's important to take the newfound knowledge you acquire from this book and weave it into a working trading tapestry for yourself. The truth is, all successful traders eventually mold the rules to their individual trading style; this takes time and fine-tuning.

When I think of my own trading life in the past two decades, the one thing I would change is to have taken more risk and to have been more disciplined at the same time. So learn from the Maniac Trader. Use these guidelines and rules as your trading foundation, and you'll be well on your way.

Remember to ask questions—always ask questions. Have clear trading objectives and, most of all, have trading rules that you understand and will follow. Trading the commodity markets isn't difficult if you have the right guide, are willing to take the time to learn the ins and outs, and are not afraid to take risks.

CHAPTER 6

FORWARD THINKING

WINNING THE WAR BEFORE FIRING THE FIRST SHOT

One of the best skills I bring to the trading table is my uncanny ability to foresee the future. No, I do not possess any special spiritual gifts—at least none that I'm aware of. And no, I don't have some crystal ball on my desk or a deck of commodities tarot cards—none of these. I have many readers who believe that I do, though, and they often ask, "How do you do it?" Simple—I think ahead and I also look at history. There's an old saying, "The only news you don't know is the history you haven't read," or something like that.

Trading is no different. It's imperative to study at least some history of a market to learn what it may, or even most likely will, do. I don't mean learning about how it was founded and who its founding members were—not that kind of history. While that may be interesting, it will do little to help your trading. The kind of history I'm talking about is price history.

Using charts, we can see patterns—long, short, seasonal, and so on. If we can identify these patterns and pinpoint what preceded them and what immediately followed them, we have a good road map for the future. The famous disclaimer "Past performance is no guarantee of future results" applies here; past history does not guarantee that the future will be the same. But knowing what has typically happened throughout the history of a particular commodity can lay the groundwork for a good trading plan.

PLAN YOUR TRADES, TRADE YOUR PLANS

You can't know where you're going unless you have a plan to get there—I truly believe that. So many new commodities traders jump into these markets with no real plan or objective, and often they wind up out of the market just as fast as they got in. It's vital for every trader to have a well-thought-out and concise trading plan in order to succeed. The short time it takes to sit down and write out a well-thought-out trading plan pays for itself over and over again. I'm proof of that.

A trading plan should include your basis for trading the particular commodity in the first place. For example: I'm buying orange juice because I believe there'll be a hard freeze this winter and juice will go higher. It can be as simple as that. But to back up my trade in orange juice, I would also investigate the crop condition and the overall global demand. Then I would turn to my technical charts and see where support and resistance are for the juice and how much open interest there is. If all of these things supported my trading decision, then I would proceed.

Let me stop right there. At some point in the analytical process we all must decide whether to pull the trigger on a trade. It can be hard. Anyone can analyze any trade to the point of not being able to do anything. They call this *paralysis by analysis.*

I do certain things each time I trade, sometimes more and sometimes less. And then once I've done them, I either go through with the trade or I don't, and I quickly move on. Once you have a trade in motion, you go from that tough time of deciding what to do to managing what you have in place. Knowing ahead of time that almost all positions will go against you at some point relieves a lot of the pressure of having to always be right, right away.

So I make my best determination and then make the trade. Now I need to manage it.

You must make a plan ahead of time that lays out your exit and, in the case of a losing position, where you get out with a stop order. Never forget that this is *your* trading plan and you *must* use it. Sit down and create an action plan by first writing out a simple pros-and-cons list for a particular trade.

Next, do your research using five or six of your favorite web sites, newsletters, or other sources. Find out all you can to support your trading decision, and learn the argument on the other side, too. Once you've done that, study a chart for the particular commodity and see where it's been trading and where it was trading at this same time in the last two years. Now pick a firm entry point and exit point. Also, be sure to set two profit objectives, which we'll call PT = 1 and PT = 2. It's always good to have two profit targets, especially if you're trading more than one position at a time. Write all of this down, and do this each time. This is your action plan—a contract, if you will, a contract with yourself, and no one else. This process is vital for any successful trader. One of the first lessons I teach new traders is that you must have a plan to trade! Thus, the wise advice: Plan your trades and trade your plans.

Time Is on Your Side

Futures are called "futures" for a reason . . . time! In futures and options we're always keeping an eye on Father Time, tick, tock, tick, tock. Option prices are strongly based on how much *time value* is left in a particular option. As that option comes closer to expiration, the time value decays daily, eroding the option's value. Both futures and options expire when their time runs out, so it's vital to pay close attention to time. With options we especially need to pay attention to the time value because each day the value of the option decays a little more and so does the premium, since time value is part of the premium. Time value is always an important factor to consider when buying options.

As traders, we need to decide whether we want a longer-term trade or a shorter-term trade. As I've said, I typically like to trade futures with at least three full months to expiration, because I want the trade to have time to develop. On the longer-term trade I go no more than 18 months, because any further out, the market becomes too illiquid.

Examine each trade individually to figure out the merits of trading it longer term or shorter.

Say I believe that corn is in a long-term bull market as a result of ethanol demand, and even though (for the sake of argument) the corn is abundant right now, in 18 months it may not be; so I would buy futures expiring 18 months from now, hoping for a big move upward. Alternatively, if I thought that the Federal Reserve was planning to raise rates, I might sell gold short on a short-term basis of, say, three months. You get the idea.

Okay, time is a key factor in futures and options trading—but not the only one. One other factor that's crucial is seasonal patterns.

For Everything There Is a Season

Next to time value, knowing the seasonal factors for a particular trade or commodity is key. If you don't know that unleaded gasoline is more important in summer and that heating oil is important in winter, hang it up right now. Those examples may seem pretty obvious, but when is the key season for soybeans? Not sure? What is old crop versus new crop cotton? These are the kinds of questions a savvy trader needs to ask.

Smart traders look at seasonal charts for specific commodities, especially the agriculturals. One of the best sources of information for traders in the agricultural sector is the good old *Farmers' Almanac*. It is loaded with years' worth of data and predictions based on that data. Also, good seasonal traders follow the various crop reports for each commodity and track the weather closely. These same basic rules apply to the energy markets, the tropical markets (sugar, orange juice, cocoa), and the cattle markets. Actually, most commodities are subject to significant seasonal patterns, and it's important to know what those may be, even if they don't apply in every case. Learn the seasonal patterns and their potential effects, and then take them into account before initiating a trade.

Don't Break the Bank

Once you pick a time frame and know the seasonal patterns, you're ready to talk about risk. Risk tolerance is simply a way of saying how much you can afford. Risk varies with each trader's individual goals and investment objectives. Some good rules of thumb are easy to figure out, though—just use common sense. Simply put, don't spend out of your comfort zone. Again, that varies for everyone; you'll quickly figure out yours. For example, trading corn futures is far less prohibitive than, say, trading S&P 500 Index futures. As we've seen earlier, corn requires only a few hundred dollars of initial margin, while for S&P futures you'd have to ante up several thousand. Each commodity has its own margin requirements. Another thing to keep in mind is that some commodities move more quickly than others, exposing the trader to more rapid risk as prices change and volatility increases.

I've observed that when people trade beyond their comfort zone they begin to make poor decisions. I have done it, too—just not recently. Another way to trade beyond your comfort zone is to simply put too many positions on. If you're used to trading two positions at a time and suddenly put on 15 contracts because you feel very strongly about a particular trade, you've entered a whole different trading realm—one that may prove disastrous.

Always keep track of the equity in your trading account and never overextend yourself. Avoid margin calls—this can lead to bigger problems down the road. Simply give yourself a lot of cushion in case of adverse price moves. Not only will you make better decisions, you'll more likely sleep better at night and ultimately trade more successfully, too.

WIN/WIN STRATEGIES AND WHY PROFESSIONAL TRADERS USE THEM

The small nuances and out-of-the-box thinking that are the difference between good traders and great traders are often simple but also very important.

The Art of Selling Short

The phrase "Buy low, sell high" is a futures trader's mantra. And the premise is pretty obvious. But in commodity futures, unlike equities, it's just as easy to make money in a declining commodity as it is in one that's climbing by doing the opposite—sell high, buy low. For many new traders, this is one of the most difficult principles to understand.

In commodities, buying low and then selling at a profit later, when the price goes up, is called *going long*. When we sell a futures contract when prices are high and buy it back later, when the price has gone down, we're said to be *short the market*. There are no special requirements or extra margin needed to go short the market in commodities, and you don't have to own the actual commodity to sell it.

"But how can I sell something I don't own?" you ask. "Isn't that risky, not to mention a little shady?" No, not in futures trading. You simply elect to sell and buy back later instead of buy now and sell later; that's all there is to it. The best commodity traders take advantage of both sides of the market, frequently switching sides from long to short when the market gets overbought, and then back to long when the market gets oversold. The trick is deciding when that is.

I use this strategy all the time. One trade that comes to mind is when I bought October cattle options that were, at the time, way out of the money. I bought simply because we were heading into summer grilling season (those seasonals again!) and the cattle had been way oversold, not just in my opinion but various reports were saying so, too. The position dragged a bit but then suddenly moved higher, and then on top of that the Japanese announced that they were once again allowing imports of U.S. beef—that was the clincher. I grabbed my hefty profits, then sat back and let the market trade a bit higher. Then, as the market reached significant technical resistance, coupled with the fact that the buzz indicated that meats were overbought, I went short. The market actually moved higher for a bit and then suddenly broke down on massive selling and profit taking. Suddenly my short position was a winner!

It's imperative that a trader look at both the long and the short side of every market; forget that old mentality that you can only buy—pure nonsense. In fact, you can still be long-term bullish on a market and short it once in a while. Gold is a perfect example of a good market for this. I may believe gold is going to $2,000 an ounce, but each time it makes a new high there might be a chance for a short-term sell position. The bottom line is that if you don't trade the short side of the market as well as the long side, you're seriously limiting your profit potential. But make sure you know the arguments and reasons for both sides.

Entry and Exit Strategies: Discipline, Discipline, Discipline

Earlier I taught you about using limit and market orders as well as stop orders. All of these are ways to enter and exit a market. Discipline in trading is one thing I preach endlessly when I do training and in my newsletters—I can't stress it enough. The old saying "Practice what you preach" definitely applies. But all of us are human and can stray from what we know is right, and when we stray we usually end up paying in some form. In trading that usually means losses, or at least a lot of grief. By using a disciplined yet somewhat flexible approach, you'll find that you consistently trade better, without as much anxiety.

Each trade is different, but the same general rules usually apply. Let me repeat: Pick your entry point from your trading plan and don't chase the market; if a price gets away from you, reassess the trade or entry point. If you are using a market order, be sure to know where the market is actually trading.

When exiting a trade, set a specific trading profit level and vary from it only slightly, if at all. It's sometimes better to set your profit level just above or just under key numbers. What's a key number? A key number could be something as simple as $80 crude oil or $900 gold. Why? These numbers are main numbers in that they end in "00" and are simply key technical and psychological points that many people choose. A better selling point might be $899.50 (depending on your buy point). My point is that it's sometimes better to set your entry and exit points just shy of these more visible numbers and where a lot of traders park their orders; it gives you a bit of an edge to be filled before the others while not leaving much profit on the table.

Discipline requires that we set aside ego, which can be a killer in these markets. Discipline also necessitates that we set aside our greed for more, more, more. This is the most common pitfall for any commodities trader. It's hard, when you have 400 percent return and it's growing, to say, "Okay, my goal was to get out with these profits, so

I'm out." Most people's greed kicks in right about that time, and if they have 400 percent, they want 800 percent. They may win and win big on this trade, but if they use that mentality consistently, they'll end up with far more losers than winners. Slow and steady wins the race (if you want to call 400 percent returns slow).

In my opinion, discipline is the key and *the* objective for every commodities trader—myself included. It's the Holy Grail of trading. Many people who use expensive trading systems, or newsletters, or whatever else, have a system, and yet often they don't follow it. There's no point in having a system, or even a trading plan, if you aren't willing to follow it. It's like having a smoke alarm with a dead battery. Remember what the Maniac Trader said earlier: Plan your trades and trade your plans.

Cut Your Losses . . . and Let Your Winners Run

One of the most difficult and important skills to learn in this business is profit and loss management. This falls under the discipline category but is one of the hardest to practice because none of us wants to accept losses; it goes against our very nature. However, we need to change that. Losses are part of trading; let me tell you that right up front. Fortunately, losses have been a minor part of my career, but I've had them. In fact, I've used some of the losses from my early days of trading to teach myself what *not* to do.

One particular trade stands out in my mind. I was still pretty green and had gone short three cotton contracts when I could really only afford one. I was in over my head and was also trading a market I was not all that familiar with. To add to my problems, I was unaware that the cotton crop report was coming out that morning; before I could act and try to offset the trade, the report came out and my position was toast. The market rocketed higher and the futures went *lock limit up,* which means they can't go any further, at least not right away. So here I was, overextended, in a market I wasn't comfortable trading, with extremely bullish news—three strikes against me! I had broken my own rules and now had a losing position with no way out. Fortunately, my good friend Dave Butler advised me to spread-trade out of my position, which I did, for a smaller loss. But that little episode taught me to be much more careful in the future.

Some statistics show that 65 percent of all commodities trades will end up losers, and you can raise that number for options buyers. I believe it, because many people just trade these markets blindly, with no discipline or trading plan. But the percent ratios don't mean much to me. Let's just say for the sake of argument that I place twelve trades per year, one a month. Out of those twelve, ten lose money and two make money. Did I end the year with a profit or a loss? This is a bit of a trick question because you need more info. At first blush your answer might be that I have a loss because I had ten losing positions and only two winners. True, on paper I closed out more trades as losers than as winners.

But let's fill in a few more of the blanks. Let's say that on those ten trades I was trading corn and had an average of only about a $200 loss on each trade, for an overall loss of around $2,000 plus commission. We will call my total losses for the year $3,000. Now, let's say my two winners were in the crude oil market, where I bought at $65, and the futures go to $75. That's $10 on each contract, a very profitable move. On those two trades alone I would have made $10,000 each, or $20,000 total, less commissions. *Wow!* So net/net I would have been very profitable for the year.

It's always important to look at the whole picture when trading—don't get tunnel vision. Losses are okay, just keep them as small as you can. Again, one way to do that is by maintaining discipline and checking your greed at the door. On the flip side, when you have a winning position let it run and don't be greedy—just let the trade do its work and when it begins to slow down, take your profits. Most of all, never second-guess your entry or exit point. Too many times I hear traders saying, "I wish I would have held on longer, I wish I would have waited." Blah, blah, blah. If you decide to take profits or limit a loss, then that *is* the right decision; once you've made it, it's time to move on. Don't dwell on it; don't focus on it; pick your next trade and move along. If you apply all of this in your everyday trading, you'll consistently make more money and your path to prosperity will be much quicker and smoother.

OPTIONS PRIMER: KEEPING IT SIMPLE

Options on futures are one of the most profitable ways to trade resource commodities. Commodities have many advantages over equities and even resource equities. Why? Well, the actual commodity is the underlying intrinsic value of the futures and options contract, while a resource stock is simply a resource company, which has all the pitfalls of any company—such as boards of directors, corporate scandals, quarterly earnings misses, and strikes. Gold, in contrast, has none of these drawbacks—it's simply gold. To take it a step further, options on commodities allow you to trade as close to the underlying commodity as possible with less hassle than trading the physical commodity itself. Options also give you very high leverage and limited risk. All of this and more make commodity options a far more profitable choice for trading resources than equities and equity options.

Buying versus Writing Options

It's important to understand the main differences between buying and selling, or writing, options. When we buy options, we pay a premium. That premium is the maximum we can lose—not a penny more, besides our commissions. When we write, or sell, an option, we collect the premium from the buyer.

The big difference is that the buyer's risk is limited to only what he or she paid, while the seller's risk is unlimited, depending on where the market goes. If a position is exercised against the seller, the seller must deliver a corresponding underlying futures position to the buyer at the option strike price (more about strike prices later on). This can be a painful and costly experience.

Remember, a buyer has *the right but not the obligation;* the seller has *the obligation but not the right.* I would much rather have a right than an obligation, which is why we aren't discussing selling options in this book.

Be Aware of Greeks . . .

No, you don't have to beware of what options traders call "the Greeks," but just be aware of them and what they mean. All of these are Greek words that represent different elements of option trading:

- *Delta* is a measure of how much an option premium changes, given a unit of change in the underlying futures price. Often, delta is interpreted as the probability that the option will be in the money by expiration.
- *Vega* is a measurement of how the price of an option changes versus a change in volatility. Typically, it's expressed as a percentage of the change in volatility.
- *Gamma* is a measurement of how fast delta changes, given a unit change in the underlying futures price.
- *Theta* is a measure of the rate of change in an option's theoretical value for a one-unit change in time to the option's expiration date. In other words, it measures our old friend time decay.

It's All about Style

Options can be traded either American-style or European-style. American-style options may be exercised at any time between the date of purchase and the expiration date. Most exchange-traded options are American-style. European-style options, however, may be exercised only during a specified period of time just prior to expiration.

Exercising Your Options

Exercising your option means that the buyer uses his or her right to buy (if it's a call option) or sell (if it's a put option) the underlying security, at a specific price, called the *exercise,* or *strike,* price, that was defined in the option contract. (Strike prices are set by the exchange and have different intervals depending on the underlying contract. Strike prices are set above and below the existing futures price, and additional strikes are added if the underlying futures move significantly up or down.)

The Long and Short of It

An example of a long option would be to buy 22-cent sugar calls if the market was currently at 16 cents and you believed it was moving higher because of ethanol demand. Now, if sugar moved higher and got closer to 22 cents, your options would increase in value significantly. Conversely, if you thought sugar was moving lower, back to 12 cents, you would buy puts—this would be a short option play. The short option play is simply a bet on the fact that you think sugar prices are going lower; as they do, your short position delivers profits, exactly the same as it did on the way up.

Option Spreads

Yes, we're going to add spreading to the options mix and really muddy the waters. Relax; it's not as complex as it sounds. Say you thought sugar was going higher but were not 100 percent sure how much higher. You would use a spread, buying the 22-cent calls and selling the 26-cent calls. Selling of the strike price above would help offset the buying costs of the 22-cent call.

A commonly used options strategy is the *calendar spread*. Simply put, a calendar spread involves the simultaneous purchase and sale of options of the same class and strike price but different expiration dates. Most traders would use this strategy when they're fairly neutral on the market and want to generate additional income from their investments. They'll sell an option with a nearby expiration, against buying an option (with the same strike price) that has an expiration date that's further out.

Calendar spreads can provide a way to add value to your portfolio through your purchase of a long-term option with a reduced cost basis, provided by a near-term option that you sold. Spreads have limited risk and also limited reward, so it's important to know all the parameters up front.

Some Tactical Uses of Options

There are many types of advanced strategies in options trading, but two that stand out are straddles and strangles. If the vision of a homicidal cowboy comes to mind, don't be alarmed. These terms have nothing to do with murder or riding horses; they're merely options spread trading strategies. The terms *straddle* and *strangle* give a little insight into what these types of option positions involve.

Traders who use these positions are acting on their opinions about whether the price of the underlying commodity will move a lot, or not. If you think the commodity is going to move big in one direction or another and/or if you think implied volatility is going to rise, you would buy a straddle or strangle. If you think the commodity is going to sit still or not move very much and/or if you think implied volatility is going to fall, you would sell short a straddle or strangle.

Uh-oh, I can hear your mind spinning—this is starting to sound like furniture assembly instructions in Chinese—what the heck is implied volatility? It's a term we haven't talked about before. *Implied volatility* is a measure of the fluctuation of the underlying futures price; it's determined by using option prices currently existing in the market instead of using historical data on the price changes of the underlying. Don't worry if you're confused right now. As you trade, more situations will come up and you'll see how all of these things—the Greeks, premium, theoretical value, implied volatility, and so on—are used in practical terms. Then it will all seem very simple, which it is.

Straddles and strangles are designed to play both sides of the fence, long and short. Traders don't really care if the price goes up or down, it just has to move—that's what counts.

The typical long straddle involves being long 1 call and long 1 put using the same strike price and expiration and on the same commodity. A long strangle is a little different: The trader is long 1 call at a higher strike and long 1 put at a lower strike in the same expiration and on the same commodity. This strategy is profitable if the commodity price moves up or down and significantly past the strike prices of the strangle. Now, the *really* good news is that long straddles and strangles have limited risk but unlimited profit potential, just like outright options.

So why doesn't everyone do it if it's such a license to print money? Simple. Straddles and strangles can be expensive to buy, and if the commodity price just sits there, or moves very little, losses can be significant.

I use both of these strategies, but sparingly and only when I see a significant trading opportunity. Otherwise, trading them all the time simply erodes your equity—and don't forget that commissions take a bite, too.

Now a word about selling or shorting straddles and strangles. Selling straddles and strangles can be attractive, but it's always dangerous. Just as a long straddle can lose money at an alarming rate when the commodity price doesn't move at all, a short straddle makes all the money in that scenario. But those gains can disappear in a flash if the commodity price moves too much. *Trader be warned:* Potential losses on short straddles and strangles are unlimited. Being short straddles and strangles is too dangerous for almost all but the most experienced and well-capitalized trader who understands and can employ defensive tactics quickly if things go haywire.

Always carefully consider and be sure to fully understand any strategy—basic or advanced—before using it, or it could end up costing you more then it ever might have been worth. Heed this advice: "When in doubt, stay out." See Table 6.1.

Table 6.1 Examples of Straddles and Strangles

Long Straddle	
Long 1 XYZ Sep 50 call @ $2.00, Long 1 XYZ Sep 50 put @ $1.75	
Total cost	Option premium paid, $375
Maximum loss	Option premium paid, $375
Maximum profit	Unlimited potential

Short Straddle	
Short 1 XYZ Sep 50 call @ $2.00, Short 1 XYZ Sep 50 put @ $1.75	
Total credit received	Net option premium received, $375
Maximum loss	Unlimited potential
Maximum profit	Net option premium received, $375

Long Strangle	
Long 1 XYZ Sep 40 put @ $1.00, Long 1 XYZ Sep 60 call @ $.75	
Total cost	Option premium paid, $175
Maximum loss	Option premium paid, $175
Maximum profit	Unlimited potential

Short Strangle	
Short 1 XYZ Sep 40 put @ $1.00, Short 1 XYZ Sep 60 call @ $.75	
Total credit received	Net option premium received, $175
Maximum loss	Unlimited potential
Maximum profit	Net option premium received, $175

SUMMARY AND CONCLUSION

Successful commodities trading is about thinking ahead, but at the same time remembering the past. If you can do this, you're already a long way toward formulating your trading plan. But the best trading plan is worthless if you create it and then promptly forget about it. It's like having a huge backlog of free airline miles (and believe me, I know how that goes)—you have to use it or you lose it.

Many of the things we discussed in this chapter lead back to that trading plan:

- See the big picture—no tunnel vision.
- Know that almost all positions will eventually move against you; you don't always have to be right, and believe me, you won't be!
- Once you make a trading decision, pull the trigger, then move on.
- Learn to manage your trades; figure out your entry and exit points.
- Keep time on your side; determine what works best for you in each trade—a long- or short-term time horizon.
- Everything has a season—learn the seasonal patterns for each commodity you trade.
- Discipline is the name of the game and should be the key objective for every commodities trader.
- Don't trade beyond your comfort zone—it's a guaranteed road to failure.
- Losses are part of trading; just try to keep them small and infrequent.
- Keep in mind that most winning strategies have a losing side as well.

Remember, you can't know where you're going unless you have a plan to get there. In this case, "there" is where the profits are, and where you want to be.

CHAPTER 7

THE TREND IS YOUR
FRIEND . . . UNTIL
IT ENDS

Every sunken ship had a chart.   —ANONYMOUS

TECHNICAL TREND TRADING: DECIPHERING
THE MIXED MESSAGES OF TRENDS

From this chapter title, you may be thinking that I'm a strict funda-
mentalist (not in the religious sense, but in the trading sense). Traders
often are classified as either technical or fundamental. I think that's
nonsense. Traders are either good or they're not—that's how I classify
them. I guess if I had to choose a side to be on (which I don't), I
would pick fundamentals for commodities. But the truth is, I use both
every day and for every trade, hands down. Both are important to
learn, understand, and use each and every time you initiate a trade.

The Case for Trading the Trend

As I said in Chapter 4, prices can be counted on to move in one of
three directions—up, down, or unchanged. A market trend is the
movement of market prices; once this trend is established, it will generally remain that way for a while.

Trend following has been the best style of trading for the last three
decades. Why? Simply put, trend following works, and has for such a

long time mainly because trends exist and they can be traded up and down for profit. As I've said before, markets repeat certain patterns, and if you study a chart you can decipher them. It's almost like a road map to riches.

The direction of these peaks and valleys makes up the market trend. There are multitudes of variables, and for the number of people you ask for advice on this subject, you'll get as many different answers. History, however, can be a good teacher for both fundamental and technical study; never discount it.

In our terror-filled, weather-disaster, politically volatile world, the only thing that's certain is constant change. And that's definitely true in commodities. It's impossible to forecast a trend's beginning or end until it has happened. I personally claim no psychic gifts or supernatural wizardry that enables me to say, "Here's the bottom, time to buy." It's as easy to predict a trend's bottom and top as it is to predict the weather.

If you master the basics of technical analysis, you can use market changes to make money by getting in near the bottom and getting out near or at the top. As with fundamental trading, traders' capability to switch gears with the market's ebb and flow, to remain objective and disciplined, are the keys to success. It's their ability to adapt that allows technical and fundamental traders to consistently reap profits from the marketplace.

Let's Get Technical

When I first started on the trading floor many, many years ago I couldn't even have told you what a bar chart was. At that stage of my life, I probably thought it was a ranking of the New York City watering holes. However, as I quickly learned on the floor, technical trading is an integral part of the whole open outcry and price discovery process. To repeat yet again, don't be intimidated by all the terminology—that's most important.

Just hearing the words *technical analysis* can bring to mind a NASA brain trust or that computer geek at Best Buy to whom, after listening and nodding as he rambles on, you finally just say, "Huh?" Relax. All technical analysis does is forecast the future or potential future of financial price movements based on an examination of past price movements. That's all there is to it. There are a number of ways to do it; some are more complex than others, but the underlying purpose is the same.

Let's be up front here—technical analysis does not result in 100 percent, clear-cut absolutes about the future. It merely helps investors whittle down the possibilities of what is likely to happen to prices over time. Technical analysis is not exclusive to commodities, by the way. It's used with stocks, indexes, or any tradable instrument where the price is influenced by the forces of supply and demand (on second thought, just about anything that's traded!).

Technical analysis deals with one primary element: price. Price refers to any combination of the open, high, low, or close for a commodity or any other financial instrument over a specific time frame.

Now, this is where the choices come in. Imagine technical analysis as the "all you can eat" buffet at your favorite restaurant. You can choose time frame, style of chart, special mathematical studies, and so on. You can even go back for seconds if you like. It's just one big smorgasbord of information. Time frame, for example, can be based on intraday (1 minute, 5 minutes, 10 minutes, 15 minutes, 30 minutes, or hourly), daily, weekly, or monthly price data and last a few hours or many years. Some technical analysts include volume or open interest figures with their study of price action.

Choosing the type of chart you want to use in the first place can be daunting. I personally use simple hi/low/close or bar charts the most. However, some traders are masters at what is known as candlestick charts. What it comes down to, like anything else in life, is what works for you—not what works for Paul Tudor Jones, or Warren Buffet, or the Maniac Trader, or your buddy next door. You need to choose the types of charts that will help *you* trade better. While there's an element of trial and error here, it's still important to understand the different types of charts, so let's take a closer look at the most common types of technical trading.

Charting Your Future(s)

The major tools a technician uses are charts that graphically illustrate past price patterns. Of the many different types of charts involved with technical analysis, three stand out as the most common: candlestick charts, bar charts (hi/low/close) and, to a much lesser degree, point and figure charts. Let's start with bar charts because they're what you see most often and they're fairly straightforward.

Bar Charts

Bar charts are simply what they sound like—a set of bars that tell you the price movement (typically, open, high, low, and close) that has taken place in the market for a given period of time, from a few minutes to a few years. The information you can get from a simple bar chart can be invaluable. This chart is by far the most widely used by technical analysts. As I mentioned earlier, it's my chart of choice. See Figure 7.1.

At first, to a new trader, a chart can look like something you see at a doctor's office—you may not even recognize whether you are holding it upside down or right side up. But once you learn how to read it, you'll see how simple it really is.

The horizontal scale on the bottom of the chart simply tells us what time frame we're looking at—years, weeks, days, minutes, or

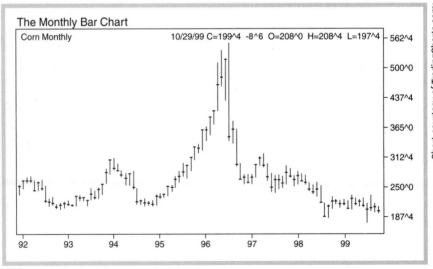

Figure 7.1 Sample monthly bar chart of Corn.

whatever. The most popular scales are the daily, weekly, and monthly bar charts.

Daily charts are most commonly used because they indicate the range of prices for one day's trade, as measured on the vertical scale of the chart. So where are the bars? Good question.

The bar is simply the range of prices for a particular time period. For example, on a daily bar chart, the top of the bar represents the highest value for the day, while the bottom of the bar represents the lowest value. If you look closely, you'll see that there are two small lines (or ticks) protruding horizontally off the bar, one on the left and one on the right. The left tick represents the opening price for the trading day and the right tick represents the closing or settlement price for the day. That's it.

So just by looking at one bar you can tell a lot. You can see where that commodity traded that day—its high, its low, its open, and where it closed, all from that one simple bar. This is why it's also known as a hi/low/close chart—it's just easier to say "bar chart," don't you think?

You can gain clear-cut information from each bit of data. When using a bar chart (or any technical analysis, for that matter), it's important not to take it piecemeal or bit by bit. All the data must be taken into account to get a clear picture.

When you combine strong, accurate fundamental knowledge and data along with the complete open, high, low, and close data, you'll have a much sharper picture of the forces of supply and demand. In a few minutes we'll talk about more complex variables you can put on any chart that can help determine even more information. But first we have two other types of technical analysis to look at.

Candlestick Charts

Candlestick trading is a true art form, and books much longer than mine are devoted to it, so my few paragraphs barely scratch the surface. I suggest that if you really find candlestick trading interesting and want to learn more, you seek out one of the many excellent resources about it. I find candlestick charts fascinating, but I'm by no means a master of them. Now let me tell you what they are.

Candlestick trading doesn't mean turning out the lights in your office and setting a romantic scene. Candlestick trading was originated by the Japanese, who began using technical analysis to trade rice in the seventeenth century. (Rough rice is still very actively traded around the world, including in the United States.)

Historians say candlestick charting first appeared around 1850. Much of candlestick development and charting credit goes to a legendary rice trader named Homma, from the town of Sakata in Japan.

Technical analysis has come a long way since Homma's time, but many things remain the same, too. Of course, his original ideas were modified and refined over many years of trading and evolved as the markets have evolved into the modern marvel they are today. The comparison may be made that an abacus still works but few people actually use them. However, just as adding machines, calculators, and computers were developed from that abacus, those first candlestick charts have become the modern system of candlestick charting we use today. Figure 7.2 shows what this type of chart looks like.

Figure 7.2   Candlestick chart.

Hold on—this looks a lot more complex than a bar chart! It's really not. The formations—and there are several—go by many different names. The basic idea remains the same, though, as we discussed. The candlestick chart helps the trader determine the price action for a specific time period. In order to create a candlestick chart, you need to have a data set with open, high, low, and close values for each time period you want to display.

The reason they're called candlestick charts is obvious: They look like candles—thicker, wider, hollow or filled bars with small wicks. The hollow or filled portion of the candlestick is called the *body* (also referred to as the *real body*). The long, thin lines above and below the body represent the high/low range and are called *shadows* (also referred to as *wicks* and *tails*). See Figure 7.3.

The high is marked by the top of the upper shadow and the low by the bottom of the lower shadow. If the commodity closes higher than its opening price, a hollow candlestick is drawn, with the bottom of the body representing the opening price and the top of the body representing the closing price. If the commodity closes lower than its opening price, a filled candlestick is drawn, with the top of the body

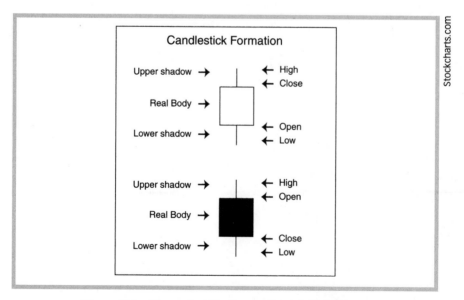

Figure 7.3 Elements of basic candlestick formations.

representing the opening price and the bottom of the body representing the closing price. I'm not going to get too much deeper into candlesticks, as I could go on for about 40 chapters. Again, if this is interesting to you, then you should absolutely seek out one of the many great sources of learning candlesticks both in print and online or even in seminars. See Figure 7.4.

Strict candlestick traders would never use a bar chart. They feel that candlesticks are more visually appealing and simpler to interpret, providing an easier-to-decipher picture of price action than bar charts or point-and-figure. The thinking is that a trader immediately can see and compare the relationship between the open and close as well as the high and low.

The relationship between the open and close is considered vital information and forms the basis of candlesticks. Hollow candlesticks, where the close is greater than the open, indicate buying pressure. Filled candlesticks, where the close is less than the open, indicate selling pressure.

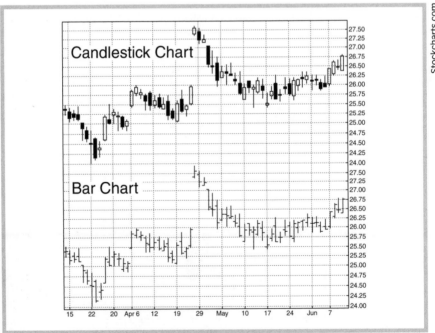

Figure 7.4 Comparison of candlestick chart and bar chart.

As I've said, traders generally choose to use bar charts or candle-stick charts in their analysis. But one other charting method bears mentioning.

Point-and-Figure

While point-and-figure charting is not as well known or often used these days, it has some unique advantages over the more widely employed charting methods. This technique became popular in 1948, when A. W. Cohen published his book on point-and-figure. Interestingly, the methodology has hardly changed since then.

When I first started on the trading floor I worked in the Dollar Index pit. There was this old-timer (probably the age I am now!) who sat in the corner of the pit all day and just made point-and-figure charts on a clipboard, using graph paper. I thought he was totally bizarre; I never took the time to understand what he was doing. Then one slow day (yes, they do happen!), I was bored and I asked him what it was all about. He walked me through what he was doing and why. I was fascinated. Confused at first, but fascinated.

A point-and-figure chart tracks daily price movements without factoring in the passage of time. Point-and-figure charts are made up of a specific number of columns that are marked with a series of stacked X's or O's.

The X's are used to illustrate a rising price, while O's represent a decline in price. This type of chart mainly filters out nonsignificant price movements and enables the trader to examine, in simple form, critical support and resistance levels. Once the price moves beyond identified support/resistance levels, the trader can place his or her trade. See Figure 7.5.

As time goes on, additional points are added to the chart once the price changes by more than a specific amount (known as the *box size*). For example, if the box size is set to equal one and the price of the asset is $20, then another X would be added to the stack of X's once the price goes beyond $21. Each column consists of only one letter, either X or O, never both. Additional columns are placed to the right of the preceding column and are added only when the price changes direction by more than a specific reversal amount.

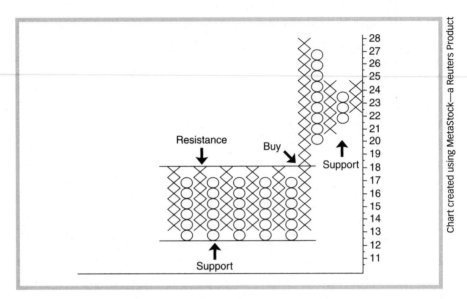

Figure 7.5   Sample point-and-figure chart.

Point-and-figure charts are mainly for long-term investment. Traders who swear by them call point-and-figure charts one of the simplest systems for determining solid entry and exit points, hands down. In my opinion, the P&F monitors supply and demand of each commodity while keeping a keen eye on developing trends.

While point-and-figure charts offer a unique approach, I personally find bar charts and candlesticks are more effective—just my opinion.

The question of what type of charting method is best is similar to the ongoing one about technical versus fundamental analysis. The answer is, they're all good in their own specific ways. What it comes down to is how well does it work for you? Which one do you feel most comfortable using? These should be the determining factors for you.

But no matter what charting method you choose, you need to be able to interpret the patterns, or the whole exercise is pointless.

Chart Patterns in Plain, Simple English

Knowing how to read a chart and interpreting that information into something you can use are two very different and important skills. In addition to charting, technicians have a host of other tools at their disposal. Many technicians look for specific patterns and also study moving averages and things like volume and open interest, which show the trader market momentum and strength. Technical studies such as Bollinger Bands simply and easily show where support and resistance are, so you can easily determine when a market may be getting overbought or oversold. There are many of these types of studies out there. It's a good idea to become familiar with them—they can all teach you something.

The beauty of technical analysis lies in its versatility. You don't need to be a rocket scientist to analyze a commodities chart. Charts are charts. It doesn't matter if the time frame is five days or five years. It doesn't matter what commodity or financial instrument you're charting. The technical principles of support, resistance, trend, trading range, and other elements can be applied to virtually any chart. Don't get me wrong, this is not always simple, but once someone teaches you and you practice, practice, practice, the picture will become much clearer. As with anything in life, victory and profit require serious study, hard work, and an open mind.

Chartists use a number of terms and patterns to describe the various market/price conditions, including these:

Uptrend: This tells us when the market is moving higher. See Figure 7.6.

Downtrend: This is the exact opposite of the uptrend and shows us when a market is moving lower. See Figure 7.7

Support: Support is the price level at which demand is thought to be strong enough to prevent the price from going lower. As the price declines toward support and gets cheaper, buyers are more inclined to buy and sellers are less inclined to sell. By the time the price reaches the support level, demand will generally overcome supply and prevent the price from falling below support.

Resistance: Resistance is the price level at which selling is strong enough to prevent the price from rising any further. As the price advances toward resistance, sellers are more inclined to sell and buyers are less inclined to buy. By the time the price reaches the

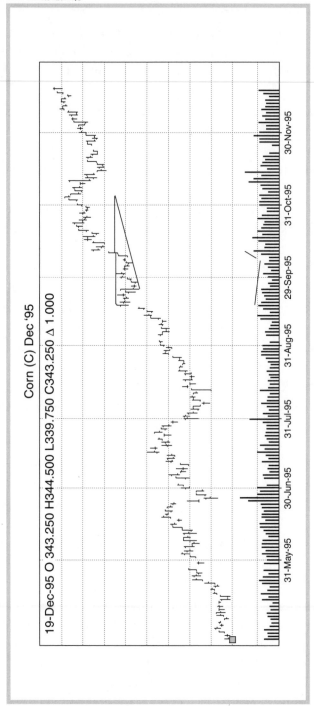

Figure 7.6 Ascending triangle pattern.

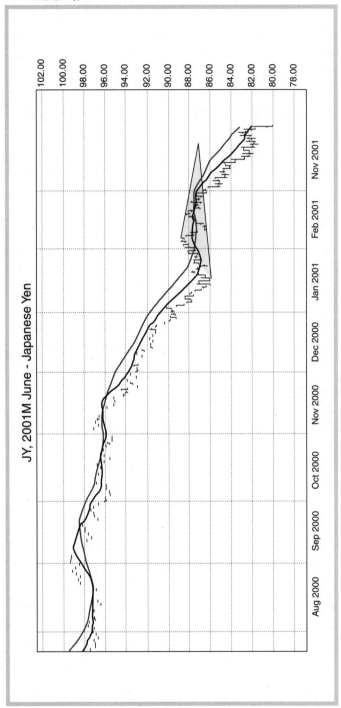

Figure 7.7 Descending triangle pattern.

127

resistance level, supply will overcome demand and prevent the price from rising above resistance. See Figure 7.8.

Breakout: No Clearasil needed here. A breakout occurs when prices pass through, and stay through, a support or resistance area. A breakout is a key factor for technicians, as it's a clear signal like waving a checkered flag at the start of a car race—time to get going! When a trend has been in a virtual holding pattern for a period of time and a breakout occurs, it's a clear signal that a new trend is in the works.

The Fancy Stuff

There are many, many other formations and patterns in the technical analysis world, and, again, there are whole volumes concentrating on them. Try to find one that explains these formations in plain English. To whet your appetite, here are two examples of more complex formations. These show up in both candlestick and bar charts, but primarily in bar charts. (Candlestick charts have hundreds of different patterns, all with unique names, which you can find out if you delve more deeply into them.)

Flags: A flag charts a straight up or down move in a commodity depending on what the market conditions are. This movement is often nearly vertical and at the very least is extremely steep. The move is so rapid, in fact, that on a daily chart a trendline can't be drawn. See Figure 7.9.

Pennants: These have nothing to do with the World Series. They're similar in structure to flags. Pennants have converging trendlines during their consolidation period. In other words, the support and resistance levels tend to meet when the market is consolidating. If a trader is trying to determine a breakout, the pennant should have weakening volume, followed by a large increase in volume during the breakout. See Figure 7.10.

Pros and Cons of Technical Trading

Just as with fundamental analysis, technical analysis is an indication of our own wants and desires. Each individual's personal biases or wishes

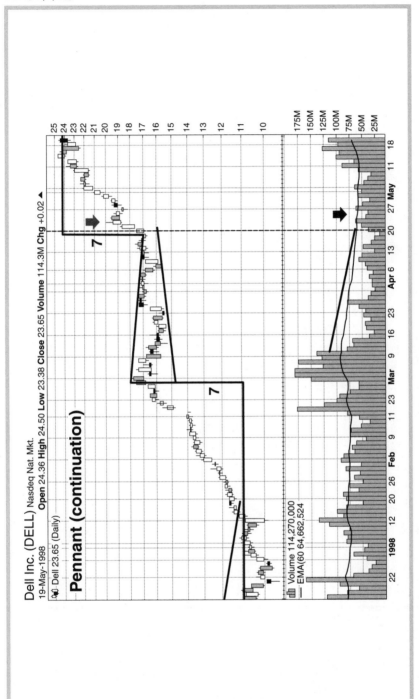

Figure 7.8 Pennant pattern.

129

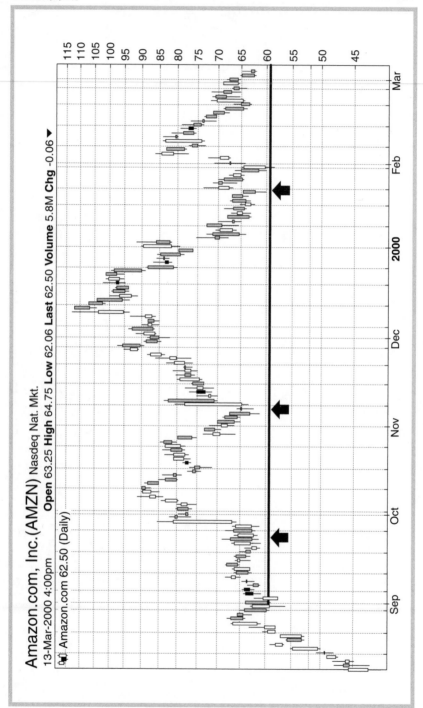

Figure 7.9 Technical support.

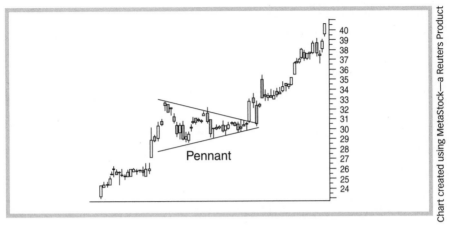

Figure 7.10   Sample pennant formation.

can be reflected in the analysis—this happens all the time. As I've mentioned before, in the industry we call it *talking your book*. It's called that because a trader may have positions on and be in a form of delusional denial of clear evidence and patterns, but is simply saying what he or she wants the market to do rather than looking at what it's actually doing.

It's important to be aware of these biases when analyzing a chart. A big red flag for me is when someone is a perpetual bull; then a bullish bias will almost always overshadow the analysis. However, if the trader is a doom-and-gloom perma-bear, then I can predict that the analysis will have a bearish tilt. The trick is to stay neutral and objective. It's not as easy as it sounds, even for the Maniac Trader.

Too Little, Too Late?

One giant criticism of technical analysis alone is that it's often simply too late to be of any use. By the time the trend is clear to the trader, the train has already left the station, so to speak. In other words, most of the move has already taken place. After such a large move, the reward to risk ratio is not as good and, therefore, is far less desirable.

One other big dilemma is that not all technical signals and patterns work. When you begin to study technical analysis, you'll come across an array of patterns and indicators with rules to match. For instance, one standard rule is that a sell signal is given when the neckline of a head–and–shoulders pattern is broken. (Huh? Don't worry, just more jargon. A head–and–shoulders pattern has nothing to do with dandruff treatment. It's considered one of the most reliable patterns indicating a major reversal of market direction, and is most often found in uptrends. Its opposite, the inverted head and shoulders, occurs in a falling market.) Even though this is a rule, it's not carved in stone and can be subject to other factors such as volume and momentum. In that same vein, what works for one particular commodity may not work for another. See Figure 7.11.

Another example: A 20–day moving average may be a great way to identify support and resistance for the S&P, but a 70–day moving average might work better for natural gas. Again, it comes down to flexibility. Even though many principles of technical analysis are universal, each commodity has specific qualities. The trader must know them, or technical analysis is useless and may even be harmful.

Avoiding Tunnel Vision—Don't Just See
What You *Want* to See

To me, the best advantage of technical analysis is that it can help with timing a proper market entry point and, eventually, an exit point. As

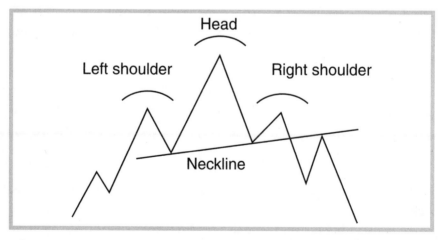

Figure 7.11   Head and shoulders as a reversal pattern in an uptrend (bearish).

I've said, it's always important to plan both your entry and your exit from a trade to avoid getting trapped. The last place you want to be when you're in a trade is somewhere like that famous old TV commercial for roach motels—you can get in but you can't get out. It's important to remain objective. It's easy to say, but really, really hard to do.

The best test is to have someone else to consult. Ask your broker or a friend or go online to chat rooms. Subscribe to a newsletter. Investing takes some work, after all—if you want to do well, that is. Having another set of eyes look over the chart from a nonemotional standpoint will be the best way to confirm or deny what you're seeing. Denial ain't just a river in Egypt; as a trader, if you're not open to listening to others, you really may be missing out.

STRIKING A BALANCE: CREATING HARMONY BETWEEN TECHNICAL AND FUNDAMENTAL ELEMENTS OF TRADING

Because I'm known to use a combination of technical and fundamental analysis, I'm continually asked what percentage of my trading is technical and what percentage is fundamental. I can tell you that, in my opinion, technical analysts consider the market to be 80 percent psychological and 20 percent logical; fundamental analysts consider the market to be 20 percent psychological and 80 percent logical. We always want 100 percent of the information. Whatever side of the argument you fall on is irrelevant because to equal 100 percent we need both. There's nothing wrong with following a trend or finding support or resistance for a trade; in fact, it should be a requirement for each trade. This information is vital. However, trading strictly off of technical patterns and charts is as foolish as ignoring them altogether.

One thing that nobody can dispute is the current price of a commodity. I mean, it's there for everyone to see. Commodity trading is based on the open outcry, free market system, as I talked about at the beginning of this book. The price set by the free market reflects the sum of the knowledge of all participants. That includes technical and fundamental traders and everything in between. These traders have researched, scanned, studied, and looked at everything from A to Z. Once a trader does that, it's time to decide to settle on a price at which to buy or sell.

In the futures markets, the forces of supply and demand are always at work. Using either type of analysis and examining price action helps us to determine which force is prevailing. Technical analysis focuses directly on the bottom line: What is the price? Where has it been? Where is it going? Fundamentals, which we'll talk about more in Chapter 8, deal with what might happen or raw data that may affect price now or in the future.

Technicians can argue that they have a very exact set of rules—to the point that they view this method as a science. I believe the opposite to be true. I see technical analysis as an art form rather than a science. As with all art, technical analysis is subject to interpretation, and often what one person finds amazing, another will find appalling. Remaining flexible while using technical analysis is the key to consistent success in trading under any conditions.

Many traders, myself included, use fundamental analysis to decide *what* to buy and technical analysis to decide *when* to buy.

In trading, timing is everything and can mean the difference between a trade in the win column and one in the loss column. By using technical analysis, traders can clearly see demand (support) and supply (resistance) levels as well as breakouts. Simply waiting for a breakout above resistance or buying near support levels can improve profits.

When to Use Only Technicals or Fundamentals,
in Which Markets, and Why

Throughout this chapter I've stressed that good integration of technicals and fundamentals is a key to prudent trading and consistent success. I'm not Gandhi—hardly—so it's not my job to make peace between the hard-core technicians and the ultraroyal fundamentalists. I'm simply saying that in most cases using both technicals and fundamentals is the best approach. In some situations, however, it's better to use one indicator over the other. But when, and in which markets?

In certain markets that are moving with lightning speed, that have extreme volatility, or that are simply waiting for major market news, technicals may go right out the window. Why? Well, the data can be skewed or flawed because of the rapid and erratic price movements; false patterns may emerge or be extremely difficult to decipher. This type of confusion has been more and more common lately as volumes and volatility have increased.

Strict technicians will pooh-pooh my comments and say that the rules of the technical approach remain the same under any market condition; while that may be true, the data itself does not stay the same. Take the gold market—lately we've had some days of $20 moves and erratic buying and selling that are hard to decipher on a chart. This can seem to indicate an overbought or oversold condition that on a normal, fairly steady market like, say, cotton would be clear, but not for gold. Alternatively, there are times when technicals are the best way to go and fundamentals may be out of whack.

For example, let's say we're trading crude oil and the weekly inventory numbers come out on Wednesday. They're mixed or unclear— now what? This is when we want to turn to our technicals to see where the support and resistance are, and observe from the open interest how many people are long and how many are short. The technicals will be our best guide for that day's trading because the locals and others are going to have no fundamental data of substance to work with; they'll have to rely on "the other side."

Again, the best course of action for a trader is to use both technicals and fundamentals, but determining which may be more appropriate for a particular situation takes practice.

CONCLUSION

Technical analysis can be the best tool you can use, or the worst. It all depends on your understanding of its advantages and limitations. While many traders, myself included, can attribute a good portion of their success to the wise use of technical analysis, anyone who says that this is the only way to go is operating with one eye closed and one hand tied behind his or her back. Keep an open mind, and remember that mastering and using technicals are only part of a good trading strategy.

As I've said repeatedly, each investor should use only that which suits his or her personal style. Believe me, that isn't going to happen overnight, and a lot of trial and error is involved. That's okay. Begin the process. Developing a style takes time, effort, and dedication, but having a technical analysis system that you can rely on at your fingertips is one of the greatest tools you can put in your trader's toolbox. Remember, though, that it's not the only tool. There's an old saying among savvy technicians: "Never go against fundamentals." We'll find out why in Chapter 8.

CHAPTER 8

UNTANGLING THE TRICKY FUNDAMENTALS OF RESOURCE TRADING

FUNDAMENTALLY SPEAKING . . .

Now that we've seen some of the benefits and drawbacks of technical trading, it's time to look at the other side (or, as some technicians see it, the dark side): fundamental analysis. Remember, as we discussed in Chapter 7, there are two basic approaches to market analysis. One is technical analysis (of market data) and the other is fundamental analysis (of market environment).

Simply put, fundamental analysis is the study of the underlying factors of supply and demand for a specific commodity. The theory is that the price of a commodity represents the point where the demand for it and the supply of it meet, or are at an equilibrium. As I mentioned in Chapter 3, fundamental factors include weather and geopolitical events in producing countries—outside forces that influence price action. For the financial futures markets, factors such as Federal Reserve actions and economic reports are key forces affecting prices.

Fundamental traders forecast price movements of individual commodities, or even entire sectors, simply by looking at various supply and demand forces. Because there are hundreds of supply and demand factors present at any one time, the fundamental analyst builds economic models to reduce the number of these variables to a few leading forces. These models are only as effective as the analyst's ability to identify dominant supply and demand factors.

FUNDAMENTAL FORCES AT WORK: USING FUNDAMENTAL ANALYSIS TO EXPLAIN AND FORECAST MARKET ACTION

It's been my experience that fundamental analysis not only can explain what *is* happening, it also can help us predict what *will* happen, depending on the economic variables used. It's important to note that forecasts are only as strong and effective as the data used to make them. A large amount of fundamental data, no matter how accurate the estimates, is based on samples. The estimates usually are subject to constant, unending revision. Strict technical traders raise a red flag right here. They all claim that fundamental analysis is flawed to the extreme because of the constant revisions. That argument will not be settled in this book.

As I told you in Chapter 7, I believe a harmony between the two is the best path to prosperity. There are just tons of fundamental reports to look at. Some reports, however, are fairly useless, and it's important to know which ones to pay attention to and which ones you can pass up. Let's look at some of the vital ones to be aware of.

Finding and Following the Most Common Fundamentals

There is simply an unlimited supply of fundamental factors to look at when trading commodities. Remember, each commodity has its own unique fundamental factors, and some employ the same ones. In other cases, some fundamental factors can affect virtually all commodities and the economy in general, but not every commodity will be affected in the same way.

I've mentioned some of the most commonly used fundamental factors in this section; this is by no means a complete list, but it will give you a good starting point. As you gain more experience, you'll be able to identify more and more fundamental factors that can impact your trading each day.

Federal Reserve Decisions and Interest Rates

The Federal Reserve, or "the Fed," as it's known to most Americans, is a government department that's kind of like the financial captain of the ship in the U.S. economy. The concept is simple—the Fed is supposed to implement policies that are designed to keep the United States operating smoothly. Again, as we all know, this doesn't always happen. Regrettably, most investors don't understand how or why the government involves itself in the economy; many feel it would be better if it didn't. Regardless, it's important to understand how it works for your own information, and also because everyone else who's trading is probably watching the Fed, too.

The Fed is more or less the bank of the U.S. government—the "banker's" bank—and it regulates the nation's financial institutions. The Fed reigns over the world's largest economy and is clearly one of the most powerful organizations on the planet. Some feel the U.S. president is far less powerful than the Federal Reserve chairman, and I agree.

It's vital for a commodities trader to have at least a basic knowledge of the Federal Reserve system. After all, the Fed dictates economic and monetary policies that have profound impacts on individuals in the United States and globally. Once you learn the basics of this fundamental you'll find the results of the Federal Open Market Committee (FOMC) rate meetings much more interesting and, it's hoped, profitable.

Commitments of Traders Report

Each investor has a favorite report. As a lifelong commodities trader, mine is this one. Simple, to the point, useful, and accurate, the *Commitments of Traders* (COT) report is by far one of the best indicators to help commodity traders determine market direction. It's published every Friday by the Commodity Futures Trading Commission (CFTC).

This government agency's mission is to regulate and enforce the laws and ethics of all commodity futures trading. The CFTC also provides investors with up-to-date information on futures market operations and is instrumental in maintaining the transparency and integrity of the markets.

The COT report provides valuable information about changes in the position commitments of various types of investors and end users, and breaks down the open-interest positions of all major commodity contracts that have more than 20 traders involved.

By analyzing this report, traders are able to determine the likelihood of a trend continuing or coming to an abrupt end. Long and short positions are calculated as well as changes from the previous week's positions. Rumor has it, as I write this, that the CFTC is thinking of ceasing to publish the report. This has caused quite a stir, and by the time you read this book they may have already done it; that would be unfortunate, as this is one of the most useful fundamental tools available for commodity traders.

Employment Numbers

On the first Friday of every month, the U.S. Department of Labor Bureau of Labor Statistics releases the Employment Situation Summary, or as it's commonly called, "the jobs report." The numbers found in this report are some of the most widely and closely watched by commodity traders and investors.

The jobs report provides estimates of the number of people employed and unemployed, the number of hours being worked, and a multitude of other key facts and figures that can give traders an immediate sense of what's going on in the employment sector.

Few reports carry as much weight on Wall Street as this one. The jobs report is closely monitored and discussed by economists and CEOs of Fortune 500 companies as well as by individual investors. The news media often will report these numbers widely as well, so they can have a very broad audience. The numbers most certainly can impact future business and hiring decisions made by major companies, and that in turn can affect the entire economy.

Retail Sales

Another important report that traders keep a close eye on involves retail sales numbers. Each month the Commerce Department releases the number, which includes a broad analysis of consumer spending trends. This report includes car sales, clothing, food at both grocery stores and restaurants, electronics, building materials, drugs, and numerous other items. The report is expressed as a percentage of change from the previous month and is adjusted for seasonal variations.

This can be a market mover, too. If consumers are spending less, it could indicate a recession or the start of a new trend that could be felt marketwide. Because retailers use many different commodities and industry provides much of the demand, if their business is slowing, so will their demand for things like energy, cotton, sugar, and/or gold. Almost every commodity is used in some type of retail operation, so that makes this a very big number for commodities traders.

Michigan's Consumer Sentiment Index (MCSI), a private report from the University of Michigan, is released on the 10th (except on weekends) of each month. A final report for the prior month is released on the first of the month. The MCSI is watched closely and often correlates well with the retail sales numbers. After all, if consumers aren't very confident in the economy or job security, they're less likely to go out and buy stuff—anything from houses, to computers, to cars, to shoes.

One market that can have a big impact on retail sales and consumer confidence is the energy market. The energy markets have their own unique reports.

Global Energy Demand versus Supply

Each Wednesday the Energy Information Agency (EIA) releases the energy supply report for crude oil and the products. The natural gas report is released Thursdays by the American Gas Association (AGA). Both of these are simply indicators of where market demand is for the week and also where supply levels are at. Traders use this information to decide if there is enough of the crude, the products (gasoline, heating oil, etc.), and natural gas to meet demand. Once the trader has the number in hand, the next step is to look at the other factors affecting oil supply, such as what's going on in the OPEC countries.

Geopolitical News and the World's Oil-Producing Countries

Inventory numbers are very important to traders, but equally important are the geopolitical and other fundamental forces, especially in the OPEC and other oil-producing countries. If trouble is brewing in, say, Iran, then traders' eyes shift to the long side of the market. If Venezuela starts to rumble, expect to see gas prices shoot higher, because we import refined products from that country as well as crude oil. Once traders have determined the weekly supply and demand numbers, they then look at what are known as the world's chokepoints.

A chokepoint is where oil production could get held up due to an exporting country's problems or economic or political activities. Clearly, the Strait of Hormuz and the Gulf region in general are key areas to watch.

When a pipeline, oil facility, or embassy is attacked in any of those countries, you can almost count on oil going quite a bit higher, at least initially, anyway. When central bankers discuss buying gold, you can fully expect to see the price of bullion jump and even take silver along for the ride. When weather threatens crops of any kind, you can almost certainly expect to see prices surge. Much of the time these trades are based on fear, which is why we call this the *fear premium*. We tack fear premium on top of the supply and demand numbers, and the price you're left with is the price of the crude oil or its products that are derived from it.

Crop Reports: Grains, Softs, Meats, and Others

There are a variety of crop reports for everything from orange juice to corn, and all the agricultural commodities in between. In almost any crop report or crop condition report, traders want to know the answers to the same questions: How does the crop look? What has the weather done? Is the crop salvageable? Once they have those numbers, they can try to estimate future demand, thus designing a trading strategy for the future months.

The markets can be a funny place, and the trading doesn't always follow the numbers the way traders might expect. That can cause a lot of volatility. If, for example, corn showed a weak crop and damage to the ears of corn in many states, you would expect the price to go way up. Usually it will, but not always. This is where looking at the demand side of the equation comes in. In this case let's assume that on the demand side we have some problems—demand for corn has fallen off by 30 percent in the last three months. This would offset any damage to the current crop, and even though the supply report on its face is bullish, it's offset by the other report on demand. It's imperative that you have all the metrics. But remember, the easy part is getting the numbers; deciphering them and turning them into profits is the true test.

Weeding Out What Really Matters in the Numbers

One of the most difficult and yet vital skills of a trader is being able to decipher fundamental factors and translate them into real, workable, and actionable trading strategies. This can be a lot of work but is well worth it if you're willing to spend the time and energy on it.

Knowing What Numbers to Expect and How the Market Might React

It's simply impossible to know how the market might react to a report, and it's best not to try. In my experience, it's always best to be more or less flat—holding no position going into a report or number. However, if you have a strong fundamental belief backed up by solid technicals, regardless of one set of numbers, then go for it. As I've said, if your decision to trade is based on the supply and demand as well as technical factors, you should be on firm ground. Even though the numbers at the moment might move the position against you, over the longer term, you may still be right. Certain markets are dependent on certain reports more than others.

One example is the employment report. The currency market is usually most affected by this report. In a 1995 study, the Federal Reserve Bank of New York noted several ways in which employment data impacted the currency market.

For example, they pointed out that an unanticipated rise in employment means a rise in the dollar. The study reported also that reactions to surprises are related to the implications for short-term interest rates.

The employment report's followers don't stop with the currencies. The bond market is concerned with what the report might indicate about inflation and interest rates. In this scenario a strong employment report might indicate an economy that's heating up too quickly and lead economists and traders to become concerned about inflationary pressure.

However, it can also raise concerns about tighter monetary policy and future interest rate increases. The commodity market looks for rising employment as a sign of corporate optimism and growth potential. It's also focused on inflation and interest rates to a lesser degree. How you look at it often depends on your position in the market and your personality.

Often a report's expectations are already priced into a market, as participants have already traded based on their predictions for the report. Figuring out if a report has already been priced in can be hard, but it's very important to know whether it has or not.

Analyzing Whether Fundamentals Are Already Priced in the Market

The old saying "Buy the rumor, sell the news!" is usually good advice, but not always. Most big fundamental numbers are expected far ahead of time. It's not as if traders don't know they're coming. Now, an act of terrorism, a hurricane, a refinery explosion, political strife—those things are unexpected fundamentals that can move markets rapidly because they come out of the blue; traders have no time to prepare and often have only a little information.

The numbers that come out each week and month usually come out on the same day and at the same time, so their announcement is largely anticipated. Many analysts spend their whole lives just trying to predict those numbers, and traders are bombarded by the media whenever a number is pending, as if the whole world's future depends on the coming announcement. Usually it's not so dramatic. This is where our adage comes from—the rumor is often much more volatile (and scary) than the actual facts.

For example, let's say that everyone and their mother are predicting huge drawdowns (in other words, a lot of usage) of gasoline. The EIA report comes out on Wednesdays at around 10:00 AM. If all of the market is frightened by the predictions of gigantic drawdowns the whole week before the report, the price is sure to rally. Then on Wednesday if the report comes in and shows draws (usage) were not so high, or maybe even negative, sellers will fly out of their long positions faster even than when they went in. Much ado about nothing.

Speculation is based on this type of anticipation, and you can make a lot of money just riding the rumor higher, but be sure to get out or be flat, as we discussed earlier, before the number comes out. Holding a position through a number is pretty close to gambling—not a good word in the futures industry. One way to handle it is to at least take half of your position off before the number hits, and grab some nice profits that will cover your other half of the position should it go against you.

Fair Value: Determining Maximum Upside and Downside Risk

Have you ever heard the saying "Life isn't fair"? Sure, we all have heard it and probably have said it a few times, too. As in life, trading often doesn't seem fair, either. As traders, it's our job to look for value. But what is value and how do you know if you're getting it? Well, let me compare it to something you've done before. When you went to buy your last car did you shop around until you found a good deal? Most likely you first decided on the kind of car you wanted and then compared prices. After you found out the price, you began to negotiate and then eventually purchased the car. Trading is really no different.

Our first step as traders is to pick which commodity we want to trade. Then we need to find out where the market for the futures and options is currently trading. We also need to see where the commodity has been trading recently, or even in the distant past (a long-term or seasonal chart is great for this purpose). Fair value, like so many things in life, is relative. In other words, what might seem fair to you, may not seem fair to me, so we need a model that can be a basis for everyone.

Some technical indicators and charts, along with studies like Bollinger Bands, can give traders a good indication of whether they are buying the low or the high. (As mentioned in Chapter 7, Bollinger Bands indicate when a market is overbought or oversold.)

Fair value can also be calculated by many computer programs that are available or via different trading platforms that do the calculations automatically. In particular, it's important to determine what fair value is for the options based on where the futures price is at the present time. These computer programs help you do that. Here's how you can use fair value to determine where the market will open.

Everyday before the market opens, people want to know, or at least have a general idea of, where it might come in. For example, let's say you're an S&P trader. If you're experienced, you know that the Standard & Poor's 500 futures contract, which is based on the S&P 500 Index, is a valuable forecasting tool. But what exactly is the connection between the S&P 500 Index and futures on this index, and how can this connection help define where the market will open?

Finding Value: Comparing Futures and Cash

The S&P 500 is a capitalization-weighted index with an aggregate market value of 500 companies that represent major industries. The S&P 500 futures contract is based on the S&P 500 cash index. It represents the "obligation to deliver" the value of the index on a certain future date (the expiration date).

Traders always need to look at two key factors when evaluating the S&P futures contract and the relationship between the futures and the S&P 500 Index or cash market.

When the spread between the futures and the cash price is examined, if the futures trade above the cash, then we refer to it as trading at a premium to the cash market. If the futures contract trades below the cash, it is called trading at a discount to the cash. Pretty basic, right?

To calculate the premium (discount), all you have to do is subtract the cash value of the S&P 500 Index from the value of the S&P futures contract. (This works for any commodity that fits your needs.) Take a look at the following example:

$$S\&P \text{ futures} = 944.0$$
$$Spx \text{ (Cash)} = 940.0$$

In this example, the spread, or premium, is 4.00. Once you know the premium, the next step is to determine the fair value. The formula for fair value (FV) is as follows (now remember, I told you I was never any math whiz, so don't think of it as math, but as a series of steps; if you like math, then think of it as math):

$$FV = SPX \star (1 + r) \, t/Div$$

Let's break it down so it's easier to understand.

> Spx = spot price of the S&P 500 Index
> r = interest rate on a six-month Treasury bill
> Div = Dividend sum derived from the stock owned
>   during the life of the futures contract
> t = Days remaining until expiration of the futures
>   contract (in years)

One of the best ways of determining fair value is to use the Black-Scholes model, considered one of the most important concepts in modern financial theory. It was developed in 1973 by Fischer Black, Robert Merton, and Myron Scholes and is still widely used today. The Black-Scholes model, often called simply Black-Scholes, is a representation of the varying price over time of financial instruments, and in particular stock options, but it can apply to commodities as well. Although the equations can seem very complex, it's a must-read for the new trader, even if it's just to get a sense of what the model is.

But whatever method you use to determine fair value in advance, ultimately the futures market, through open outcry, actually determines it.

MANIAC TRADER'S BEST PICKS

If you really love math and enjoy a heavy, complex read like *War and Peace*, there are many books out there that explain the Black-Scholes model. One book is *Option Pricing: Black-Scholes Made Easy* (John Wiley & Sons, 2001), by Jerry Marlow. When I started on the trading floor, my benefactor gave me several books, including one of the *War and Peace* variety; he also gave me another book at the same time—more my speed, as I am not a big reader of heavy books. If you're like me, I highly recommend *Reminiscences of a Stock Operator* (John Wiley & Sons, 2006), by Edwin LeFevre.

FUNDAMENTAL ANALYSIS THE MANIAC TRADER'S WAY

Let me share a specific instance when I used fundamental analysis and the market went against me initially, and then came back around to deliver huge profits, proving my original analysis was right. A good example that comes to mind is in the orange juice market. In 2006 the Florida orange crop was in bad shape. The harvest had been dwindling year after year, decimated by citrus disease spread mainly by hurricanes. (Citrus canker is one of the fungus-type diseases—it has destroyed millions of oranges while they were still on the tree.) Many Florida growers simply sold their groves to real estate developers because it had become so difficult to make a living. This further lowered the potential supply.

As if that weren't enough of a bullish indicator, lack of migrant workers to harvest the oranges was another problem that would likely drive prices higher; growers simply couldn't find the help they needed to harvest the oranges. The final test for me was to go to Florida myself and see the orange crop and talk to some growers. I knew after that trip that the crop was in deep, deep trouble. This was in the spring of 2006, and I bought November 175 and November 180 call options.

Over the start of the summer, the market languished a bit and my readers were nervous. But they did take profits on the 175 calls. I encouraged them to hang on to the 180 calls on the chance of a hurricane or something else.

Then the Steger Report, an independent crop estimate report, came out. Private analyst Elizabeth Steger projected 123 million 90-pound boxes for the Florida orange crop in the coming season. The crop was estimated at 160 million boxes with the possibility of 5 percent more or 5 percent less by Louis Dreyfus, the large commercial firm. The end users such as Sunkist and Tropicana, also called "the trade," were looking for a similar projection from Steger.

When the report was released, the orange market went bananas (ouch!). Juice rallied limit up a few days in a row. In that one move alone, our options jumped to over 140 percent profits. All this and not even the hint of a tropical depression, let alone a hurricane! The fundamental analysis I used had worked, and it clearly showed me ahead of time that the juice market was in trouble. One other thing I did was to look at a 10-year seasonal chart and a 6-month chart before I pulled the trigger on this trade. Fundamentals are important, but it's always a good idea to check the technicals, too.

Using Technicals to Confirm or Deny Fundamental Trades

As we discussed in Chapter 7, using technicals to back up your fundamental viewpoint for a trade is a great idea. The more tools you have in your toolbox, the better—but you should use them all. Sometimes you have many fundamental factors that point to buying a certain market no matter what, but the technicals may indicate the market is already overbought. In this instance you may want to hold off and let the market correct itself a bit; that's strictly up to each individual. Never be in a rush to put on a trade—it's a sure sign of inexperience. Your attitude should be one of calm acceptance: "If I don't get this one, I'll get the next one."

Patience is the key here. Make sure all the factors are right; having the technicals on your side is always a good idea. Once you have all your fundamental reasons lined up, take a look at a basic bar chart, add some moving averages and a simple study like Bollinger Bands, and see what's what. Then when you decide to pull the trigger you'll know what you may be up against when trying to exit the position. Nine times out of ten, if you don't seek out fair value and pay up for an option or future and then try to exit it later, you'll find it that much more difficult.

Fundamental trading is not without its faults, and as good as it's been to me, it's also burned me.

Fundamental Flaws, or How I Learned the Hard Way to See the Red Flags

There have been several times in my career when I've used the fundamentals and the market has either gone in the opposite direction from what I anticipated or the data changed further down the road and I didn't adjust my position accordingly. Sadly, I paid the price.

A couple of examples that come to mind are a heating oil spread trade I had for the winter of 2005–2006. All fundamentals pointed to a colder-than-average winter, and very low heating oil supplies. Well, it turned out the opposite. It was one of the mildest winters on record, and heating oil supplies were adequate. It ended up being the most costly trade I had done in years.

Another instance that stands out was my bet on the first Gulf War back in 1991. In my first couple of years on the floor, I thought I knew it all. It seemed obvious to me that the dollar would be the flight-to-quality vehicle if and when we attacked Iraq. For weeks I waited, adding to my position almost every day. That fateful January night, my wish came true and the dollar exploded higher. I was a millionaire, but only for a few hours. As it became increasingly clear that, yes, we had invaded but the war was essentially over, the dollar tumbled, and tumbled hard, taking my small amount of equity with it.

I was mortified.

I learned that day that you can be right and still lose money. You have to play the tape all the way through and, most of all, not be overextended. In other words, do not put on too many positions—the "too many eggs in one basket" theory. Even though I have had some losses due to fundamental indicators, usually it's been my own greed or misinterpretation that caused them.

CONCLUSION

As traders, all of us take risks every day; there's no crystal ball when it comes to trading, at least not as far as I know. Whatever the case may be, we must adapt constantly. As I've said repeatedly, being able to adjust to any set of circumstances is imperative for successful traders.

Be sure you always know what fundamental data is coming out, and when. There's nothing like having a position on, then finding out that the biggest number for the year is about to come out, and you're operating in the dark. Examine what happened in the past under the same conditions and then look at what's different now. As I said earlier, it's one thing to get the fundamental data; it's quite another to be able to decipher it. Don't be shy about asking for help at any time from your broker, a trading friend, a newsletter like mine, or from reading the many books available on the subject.

The most important things to remember are that fundamental factors are always in flux and are often released by the government—to many, that's one big strike against them.

One final thought: Just as technicians shouldn't forget the fundamentals, successful fundamental traders know never to ignore the technical signals. Remember, no single system is foolproof—a good mix between fundamental and technical analysis is the best way to go. It works for me!

CHAPTER 9

THE FUTURE
OF FUTURES

Change is in the air—and not least in the commodity markets. New products, new markets, new technologies are all coming on the scene faster than we can name them. Whoever would have thought to trade a water contract, for example? As for terrorism futures, well, even the Maniac Trader did a double take at that one! And weather futures? Come on!

One thing all commodity traders and investors wish they had is a crystal ball to predict the future. Nobody I know has one. The next best alternative is to examine history and see what commodities have worked and why, and how they evolved.

The futures markets have been around for a very long time, and are showing no signs of going away soon, if ever. In fact, the markets are seeing exponential growth and interest from investors around the globe, as most experts (myself included) believe we're on the brink of a cyclical commodities boom.

Throughout history, markets have come and gone as the needs of consumers and industry changed. What were once very actively traded commodities are now either delisted or illiquid. Futures contracts and exchanges fill a need for price discovery; once that need disappears, the futures contract usually follows.

HERE TODAY, GONE TOMORROW

Let's look at an example. Two markets that were heavily traded in the past were eggs and butter. Back in 1898, butter began trading at the Chicago Butter and Egg Board, which later became the Chicago Mercantile Exchange, Inc. (CME). (The Exchange's original 48 members would be amazed—and very pleased—to see what their shares are worth today!)

Back then, the exchange traded eggs and butter in the form of what were called *time contracts,* more commonly known as *forward contracts.* Forward contracts allowed for the delivery of a specific amount and quality of butter at an agreed-upon future date, at a specified price. Back in the beginning, the process was much more informal. Basically, the producers and potential users would get together and haggle over prices, quality, and other matters. Eventually, the traders would agree upon the transaction terms, they'd shake hands, and they would have a contract. Later, to simplify things, commodities exchanges established standard forms of contracts, which included quantity, grade, and quality, to save time and make things more uniform. These, of course, evolved into the futures contracts we know today.

During World War I, commodity prices skyrocketed, and by 1917 there were problems at the exchange—many of the butter contracts were going unfulfilled, as suppliers defaulted and went after the higher prices the market was offering, leaving the original buyers to fend for themselves. This led to the government enacting what was called the Food Control Act in 1918, which suspended the trading of butter and egg contracts immediately. That, as they say, was that. The ban was lifted in 1919, but it was too late; the damage had been done.

During this period, the Butter and Egg Board members reinvented and renamed themselves, and the Chicago Mercantile Exchange was born in October 1919. The exchange established new rules to oversee the trading of butter and eggs. As a result, trading in butter futures

CHANGING MARKETPLACE

I remember that on one of my first visits to the CME, I saw them trade butter. The process is actually more nostalgic now than anything else, as the contract is no longer actively traded. Traders love history, and the whole activity of trading butter is more for entertainment than anything else. But they do it just as they used to in the 1940s, when the exchange was located at 110 N. Franklin in Chicago.

This guy rolls out a blackboard, which is still used in the cash market trading sessions that occur every Friday morning on the CME's lower trading floor. All transactions are recorded on the board. It's all very quaint but as I've said, it's more for show than anything else.

began that following December. Also, a clearinghouse was formed to match and process the trades. Trading was now much more formalized, and also much more secure.

The real downfall for the butter contract came after the 1940s. As government support prices became more common, the need to use butter futures as a hedge against unexpected price swings almost completely disappeared. Butter futures at the CME officially stopped trading in 1976, leaving only a spot market that still trades for several minutes on Friday mornings.

Fast-forward two decades. The depletion of government stockpiles of butter and resulting cash market price volatility renewed the dairy industry's need for effective risk management tools. So on September 5, 1996, the CME relaunched butter futures and added options. Activity is still rather low-key, but the contract has come full circle, as many commodities do.

WHY DO SOME CONTRACTS FLY HIGH AND OTHERS LAND WITH A THUD?

Sometimes there's little or no logic behind why a certain commodity succeeds as a futures contract and another fizzles even before it's launched. Countless futures contracts were created with huge expectations, only to fail miserably. One example that comes to mind is the demise of diammonium phosphate, or fertilizer, futures. The fertilizer contract was touted as the next big thing and was hyped by the CME and the industry in general. Primarily, the problem was that diammonium phosphate cash and futures markets were not well linked right from the beginning.

Another major hurdle was that the initial futures contract specifications resulted in a high rate of delivery. That reduced market participation and limited liquidity. Ultimately, the contract failed because it was a poor hedging tool and the industry perception was that it did not offer benefits above and beyond what were available from trading vehicles already in place in the industry. So, due to lack of interest, it was delisted and disappeared as if it had never existed. Other notable yet pretty much forgotten futures contracts include frozen tiger shrimp at the Minneapolis Grain Exchange, broiler chickens at the CME, and the infamous ECU, or European Currency Unit, which traded (briefly) on the FINEX in the early 1990s.

Today, there's much the same hysteria about another new futures contract—ethanol. The U.S. ethanol industry is experiencing exponential growth, and this trend is expected to continue. Contributing factors are higher prices for crude oil and gasoline, relatively low prices for grain, bans on MTBE (ethanol's main competition as an oxygenate), and growing concern about national dependence on imported crude oil. In 2004, the industry produced a record 3.41 billion gallons of ethanol, more than double 2000 production. That number is expected to surge again by 2007.

The substantial growth in U.S. ethanol demand and production has further highlighted the need for price discovery and a reliable risk management mechanism. Due to poor correlations, attempts to hedge ethanol against corn or unleaded gasoline have proven to be ineffective historically. Enter the ethanol futures contract.

The Chicago Board of Trade, working with petroleum and ethanol market participants, developed the CBOT Denatured Fuel Ethanol futures contract—ethanol futures, for short. These contracts are designed as a hedging tool for buyers and sellers throughout the ethanol industry.

There's also a New York Board of Trade ethanol contract, which is sugar-based. At first this contract was doing very well, but activity fell way off when the corn-based contract in Chicago was launched. While both contracts are in their infancy, interest is growing quickly, especially as unrest in the Middle East shows no signs of abating and those prices at the gas pump keep rising.

COMMODITIES EXCHANGES: ARE THEY STILL NECESSARY?

I think we'll always need commodity futures, and even open outcry, in one form or another. The exchanges were developed as a way to have open and fair communication and a transparent marketplace. That need hasn't changed—in fact, in today's global markets, it's more important than ever. But exchanges aren't the same today as they were even a generation ago.

Let me share an example. Though the Internet has reduced the need for newspapers, most of us still read them. The electronic news media have taken a great deal of market share, but newspapers are still around and probably always will be.

The same holds true for the trading pits. In today's futures market, many commodities trade both in the pit and electronically, even side by side (at the same time). If anything, electronic trading has enhanced the price discovery process, and it's almost certain that eventually all markets will be on one electronic platform or another. However, many markets may keep open outcry in the pits, too. Just what is open outcry and what makes it unique?

The Free Market at Work: Open Outcry Evolves

When commodity futures contracts were born, exchange members traded them via open outcry, which is pretty much unique to the futures markets. Open outcry was thought to be the best way for each trader to have a fair chance to buy or sell. There were no secrets—what you heard was what you got. This system of trading—which is still used today—essentially involves hundreds of auctions going on at the same time. That's what all the yelling and hand gestures are about.

With the open outcry system, traders stand in a specific (corn, gold, crude oil, whatever) trading pit and call out prices and quantities that show their willingness to buy or sell. They use hand signals to convey the same information because it can be difficult to hear if everyone is shouting at once—like trying to talk at a rock concert.

Open outcry is an efficient means of price discovery, allowing buyers and sellers to arrive at the best prices, given the supply and demand for a given futures or options on futures contract. Over the past 20 years or so, its speed and efficiency have been further enhanced by the introduction of a variety of trading floor technologies.

Some traders have been reluctant, or actually afraid, to embrace the new technology, but ultimately it seems this is the path the markets will take if they are to grow. Floor staff and traders have been afraid that life as they know it is changing, with their job security becoming more tenuous and stressful, as fewer employees are needed at the exchanges and jobs are being eliminated.

Like anything else in the industry, open outcry has evolved to meet the needs of an ever-changing marketplace. And as I've said many times, traders must adapt to change or go the way of the manual typewriter. Often nowadays you'll see traders in the pit using handheld electronic systems for trading—the best of both worlds.

Floor versus Screen: Futures Enter the Electronic Age

When, in 1987, the CME announced that they were launching an electronic trading system, they almost got laughed out of the industry. After a number of fits and starts, CME's Globex® electronic trading platform took off in 1992, and hasn't looked back since. Right about the same time, as exchanges outside the United States considered building futures exchanges from scratch, electronic trading was seen as the way to go for cost reasons and also to inject "upstairs" trading expertise into the floor trading process. During the 1990s, almost all index futures exchanges outside the United States either started as or

SCREENS COME ON THE SCENE

I remember when I had my first seat in the Dollar Index and a company by the name of Timber Hill got permission to put a computer screen in their booth facing the pit. Their broker would see color-coded bars on the screen and that told her what to do to arbitrage her position. Traders and old-timers in the pit were very angry and felt the computer was the sign of the end of trading, and life, as they knew it. That was 1989, and trading hasn't changed, for the most part. Sure, there are many more markets that are electronic, but pit trading is still very much alive and well.

shifted to an electronic format. But given the more than 100-year legacy of futures exchanges based on open outcry trading in Chicago with a large, strong, and vocal constituency among Chicago Board of Trade and CME members, the U.S. futures markets had to be dragged, kicking and screaming, into the electronic trading age.

Modern electronic trading really started with the CME's open outcry platform and trading floor systems that are linked to the CME's Globex® electronic trading platform. Their platform allows market participants to buy and sell whether they're sitting at trading booths on the floor or halfway around the world. Electronic trading has many benefits, but some traders prefer face-to-face interaction, so the CME offers both open outcry and electronic markets—something for every trader.

Day and Night, Night and Day

Whether you do it on the floor or electronically, trading is trading. In a sense, the trading screen replaces the trading pit, and the electronic market participants replace the brokers standing in the pit. So why trade electronically? Several reasons:

- *Speed.* Average response time is measured in seconds or even fractions of seconds, while in open outcry trading, it can take from a few seconds to a few minutes to execute a trade, depending on how complex the order is. And as any trader knows, speed is of the essence.

- *Transparency/integrity.* In an electronic system, all market participants can see accurate prices virtually all the time. Trade information is sent to the clearing organization and brokerage, and
  prices are also instantaneously broadcasted to the public. State-
  of-the-art technology provides real-time, anonymous order execution and reporting.
- *Global markets.* Electronic trading knows no boundaries, whether
  geographic or time. You can sit in your office in Ohio at mid-
  night and trade with a guy in Tokyo, and not miss a beat. Traders
  around the world can trade virtually around the clock, giving
  them access to a large and always-growing liquidity pool.
- *Cost-effectiveness.* Electronic trading involves less staff, which
  means less expense. Because costs and overhead are lower to your
  brokerage firm, they usually offer much better rates for those
  individuals choosing to trade online.

Electronic Markets Down the Road

As electronic markets expand, more and more contracts are likely to be
developed and many existing ones will begin trading electronically,
too. A case in point is the Chicago Board of Trade (CBOT).

The CBOT is one of the world's oldest, and one of its leading,
derivatives exchanges. The CBOT owes its beginnings to grain trading, and the grains are still an integral part of the exchange. But as the
rest of the world markets have evolved and adapted, the grains have had
to, as well. CBOT full-sized, physically delivered agricultural futures
contracts are now traded on its electronic trading platform, along with
the traditional open outcry system, during daytime trading hours; this
is known as *side-by-side trading.*

On August 1, 2006, the CBOT began trading its corn, wheat,
soybean, soybean oil, soybean meal, rough rice, and oat futures contracts on e-cbot, the exchange's electronic trading platform, side by
side with CBOT open auction markets. This format proved to be so
popular that the exchange added its South American soybean and
ethanol futures contracts during daytime hours on e-cbot. The new
trading hours have expanded global market access to the CBOT's agricultural products, especially those in the European and Asian time

zones. In all, you can trade CBOT agricultural contracts electronically from 6:30 PM to 6:00 AM; daytime hours are from 9:30 AM to 1:15 PM (Chicago time).

Choosing Contracts to Trade Electronically

The things I look for when I'm deciding whether to trade the overnight or electronic market are pretty simple. Basically, I figure out what can affect the market in the off-hours, and what the advantage is for me to be trading a certain market electronically. I'm careful to almost always use only limit orders in the electronic markets, as the bid/ask spread can be very wide and using market orders can be dangerous.

The electronic markets provide a safe and easy way to trade some of these markets almost 24 hours a day. Certain commodities have caught on faster in the electronic arena than others. The energy markets, for example, use the day pit sessions, and then in the evening the electronic session starts, so the two work hand in hand. Other markets started as electronic only—for example, the e-mini S&P, which is the smaller size of the CME's big-daddy S&P 500 pit-traded contract. The e-mini S&P is one of the most actively traded electronic markets in the world.

Still other markets have been slow to embrace electronic trade, and these trade much more actively during the pit session—the grain markets I mentioned, for example.

As traders get more used to the electronic systems though, things will balance out even more.

COMMODITY MARKET EVOLUTION: WHAT ARE THE NEXT BIG CONTRACTS?

One new commodity class that's already on the scene but has not yet fully caught on is *single stock futures.* This contract is basically the same as a stock index futures contract; the difference is that instead of being based on a basket of 100, 500, or whatever, stocks, it's a contract to buy or sell shares of one particular stock at a predetermined price and date.

Proponents believe that single stock futures are simple, efficient tools that allow the investor to gain exposure to stock price movement without the costs of owning the securities themselves. Critics are cautioning that these new futures contracts make it easier for investors to take on potentially crippling risks. There's a little truth to both arguments, in my opinion.

The really interesting thing, in my book, is that single stock futures change the playing field, making it into a zero-sum game, with buyers and sellers equally balanced. As with the traditional futures markets, for every count in open interest, there's one winner and one loser, each with precisely matched gains and losses.

Single stock futures allow traders to take on large positions in several ways. First, the up-front costs are quite reasonable and the margins on a stock futures contract are much less than the cost of buying the stock outright.

Second, using single stock futures allows traders to play the short side of the stock market very easily. Typically, you can't easily sell a stock short on the open stock market. But the nature of futures contracts allows traders to sell stock futures short the same way they do with other commodities.

Some major exchanges that actively trade single stock futures are the London International Financial Futures Exchange (LIFFE), Euronext (formed from the Amsterdam, Brussels, and Paris stock exchanges), the Spanish Futures and Options Exchange (MEFF), and the Bourse de Montreal exchange.

For a long time, U.S. exchanges were barred from joining the wave because regulations (the 1982 Shad-Johnson agreement) banned the trading of individual stock futures. In the late 1990s, some U.S. futures firms, legislators, and regulators began complaining that the laws placed U.S. investors at an unfair disadvantage, especially in light of the anticipated increase in international access to stock futures, including some futures on U.S. equities.

The CFTC and the SEC joined forces (definitely a marriage of convenience!) to provide efficient execution and clearing of single stock futures in the United States. Today the single stock futures market is alive but not very actively traded. I personally think, however, that they're one of the potentially hottest commodity vehicles around. It's just a matter of time before the rest of the market catches on.

Terrorism Risk Futures

Over the past several years, the idea of terrorism futures seemed to be one that was developed by the government. The public reception after 9/11 was very cold and the prevailing angry mood put an end to talk of them, but the need is still there, and we may yet see some type of product evolve in the coming years. Unfortunately, the quick dissolution of this program may have suppressed an important source of information and a promising research tool.

The plan originally called for markets to price terrorism risks, and it was quickly dubbed a "terrorism futures market." The theory was not so bizarre, actually. Investors would be allowed to buy and sell contracts that would pay $100 if certain political events occurred in the Middle East. We would be able to infer from the price of these trades the probability of these outcomes. The act of pricing such risks allows us to better understand and prepare for them.

Financial markets are incredibly powerful information tools; time after time they've preceded major economic and even geopolitical events. There are many examples: The futures market in orange juice concentrate is a better predictor of Florida weather than the National Weather Service. The Iowa Electronic Markets outperform the opinion polls in predicting presidential election vote shares. The energy market weekly data has proven to be a good predictor for crude oil prices.

Another market people would love to get a better read on is real estate.

Real Estate Futures

Real estate futures are another potentially hot contract. Worried that the value of your home may plummet? Now you can bet on whether it will or not. If you don't, maybe your mortgage company or neighbor will.

The Chicago Mercantile Exchange, which deals mainly in interest rates, foreign currencies, and pork bellies, has now introduced housing price futures, based on the median home price in each of 10 U.S. cities. The futures contract isn't tailored for individual homeowners. However, it does provide some protection for mortgage companies, home builders, and anyone else with big holdings in residential real estate, if housing values shift. It also gives individual investors a way to trade the real estate market in a different fashion.

While unusual, it isn't the most exotic contract out there. The winner of that honor for the last several years has been weather futures. Yes, you heard right.

Weather Futures

Not exactly new to the scene either, but relatively unknown, are weather futures. It's estimated that nearly 20 percent of the U.S. economy is directly affected by the weather, and that the profitability and revenues of virtually every industry—agriculture, energy, entertainment, construction, travel, and others—depend to a great extent on temperature, wind, and precipitation swings.

In a 1998 testimony to Congress, former commerce secretary William Daley stated, "Weather is not just an environmental issue; it is a major economic factor. At least $1 trillion of our economy is weather-sensitive." And as we've seen with hurricanes like Katrina and drought in the Midwest, the effects of weather can be devastating.

Weather conditions tend to affect volume and usage more than they directly affect price. For example, the winter of 2005 was an exceptionally warm one; when that happens it can leave utility and energy companies with excess supplies of oil or natural gas because people need less to heat their homes. In the same way, an exceptionally cold summer in a particular part of the country can leave hotels and airline seats without occupants. Who wants to pay to travel to a cold destination for a vacation?

Weather risk is highly localized; it simply can't be defined or controlled on a broad level, even with great advances in meteorology. After all, how many times a week is the meteorologist wrong?

In the late 1990s, people began to realize that if they quantified and indexed weather in terms of monthly or seasonal average temperatures, and attached a dollar amount to each index value, they could in a sense package and trade weather. In fact, this sort of trading would be comparable to trading the varying values of stock indexes, currencies, interest rates, and agricultural commodities.

In 1997 the first over-the-counter weather derivative trade took place, and the field of weather risk management was born. An $8 billion weather-derivatives industry developed within a few years of its inception. While weather futures are not all that liquid, they're available, and are likely to get more and more active in time.

Water Futures

Water, water, everywhere, and not enough to drink. One example of this commodity already in play is at the Sydney Futures Exchange (SFE). The SFE has a market in water risk to give affected parties a tool to hedge against drought conditions, which are a very real risk in the Australian rural economy, as well as in other parts of the world.

The idea is to give farmers and individuals a series of market benchmarks, or indexes, of water availability based on the logical total of key water storage dams (known as SFE State Water Indexes). The listing of futures contracts on each regional index provides a market mechanism for parties to hedge against the future value of the index. It's the first really viable outlet for Australian farmers to hedge water risk.

The SFE water futures market is a financial market. The contracts are settled in cash; there's no physical delivery of water (no, nobody's going to dump gallons of water in anyone's backyard!). Instead, buyers and sellers have price exposure to the respective SFE State Water Index that results in realized cash profits or losses.

Water futures are almost certainly on the horizon on a U.S. exchange, and many of them have (pardon the pun) floated the idea. The need for clean water provides the global demand that will likely propel water futures into being one of the biggest commodity contracts in history.

CONCLUSION

Commodity markets fill a need—a global need—for whatever's in demand at any given time. The only thing that's certain is that those global needs are constantly changing.

The futures markets must change, too, in order to stay competitive. Never be afraid of change and never assume that a new futures contract won't work out. Remember, when the NYMEX launched heating oil, most people thought it would fail big-time. They were very wrong. Today, heating oil is one of the most liquid and effective contracts in the industry. So while water futures, weather futures, ethanol futures, or whatever is the contract du jour, sound far-fetched, they just might be the next big thing.

Never has the future of futures been so bright. These days, the need for a transparent, liquid global marketplace is more crucial than ever. We're poised on the brink of a major commodities revival, chock-full of opportunity. But as we all know, risk is opportunity's partner. And what better way to transfer, or at least reduce, that risk, than tried-and-true commodity futures? Regardless of their form, or how they're traded, they're here to stay.

CHAPTER 10

TAKING YOUR FIRST STEPS INTO THE WORLD OF COMMODITY TRADING

By now you realize that commodities can be a vital part of your portfolio. But how do you dip your toe into the water the first time? In the brave new world of commodities there's so much excitement and so much to learn. It's pretty overwhelming. But every journey begins with the first small steps. Taking those steps, however, can be intimidating. Some of the most common questions I'm asked are often the most simple to answer, and they're usually the same impediments that keep investors from trading commodities. Before I answer those questions, and more, let's do a quick review of what we've learned so far.

IN SUMMARY

We have covered a lot of ground in a short period of time; you now have many tools to help you profit in the resource markets. Let's look at what we've covered thus far.

Commodity Futures Markets Are Alive and Well

And it looks like they'll stay that way for some time to come. To outsiders, they call up visions of frenzied activity and high risk. But after a peek behind that Oz-like curtain, you'll find that these markets are a sure way—some say the only way—to capitalize on what the Maniac Trader believes will be (if it's not already) the next major commodities boom.

The world is scrambling for resources—to power our cars, to heat and cool our houses, to keep technology speeding along. At best, these resources are finite; at worst, they're well on their way to disappearing altogether. That's why now is the perfect time to jump into these markets and profit from these trends. You can realize incredible gains if you follow a few simple rules: Don't be greedy; check your emotions at the door; learn to cut your losses and let the profits ride; and above all, exercise discipline tempered with flexibility.

The commodities markets are always in flux, and it's vital to stay on top of what's new and the opportunities that brings. Do your homework! Research the markets you think you may want to trade. Be passionate about what you trade, or trading will become a chore, one that you would just as soon avoid—not a good way to make money! So be passionate about the market you choose to follow, but don't let emotions cloud your judgment.

Membership Has Its Privileges

To the uninitiated, commodity markets are a closed, arcane society, one that has its own vocabulary, dress, and psychology, all conspiring to keep outsiders out. There's definitely an element of secrecy in these markets, but once you make the effort to understand them, it's amazing how transparent they become. Learn the jargon, study the psychology, and figure out what questions to ask and you'll be on your way.

Novice or Pro?

Commodities are no different from any other business. There are the novices and there are the pros. Several things separate them; I call these the "Nots":

- Not having, and sticking to, a clear-cut trading plan
- Not taking profits—being greedy
- Not using stop orders to protect profits

- Not cutting your losses, but letting them run
- Not looking at the big picture
- Not exercising discipline
- Not reining in your emotions
- Not having enough discretionary capital; using funds that shouldn't be risked

Planning, Planning, Planning

I can't stress this enough. Everything worthwhile takes planning, and being a successful commodities trader is no different. Study the different tools available and learn which ones to use, and when. Ask for advice; people usually are happy to give it. Find a mentor; this can be a seasoned trader, a colleague on the floor, or, naturally, your broker. Find someone you trust, someone who has your best interests at heart, and use this person; that's what you're paying the person for. Figure out your entry and exit strategies and stick to them (discipline, discipline, discipline!)—don't chase the market. Determine your trading comfort zone and stay within it; it's when traders go beyond the boundaries that they end up in trouble.

The Nuts and Bolts

Without a good working knowledge of the basics, all the advice and trading plans in the world won't get you far.

- Know what you're trading; study the underlying markets and learn the supply and demand factors that drive them.
- Become proficient in the language of the market and the trading floor.
- Know the differences between futures and options, and when to use each for your best profit potential.
- Master the different market orders and when and how to use them.
- Understand the concept of margin and how it can work for you; always respect it, though.
- Learn the advantages and disadvantages of spreads before using them, and use them wisely.

- Use technical and fundamental analysis to track a particular commodity's price history and movements—remember, history repeats itself.

GETTING STARTED

I'm frequently asked, "How do I open a trading account, and why do I need one anyway?" To trade commodities and act on all you've learned, the first thing you need to do is open a trading account. Many people wonder why they need a commodities account separate from their current equities account. To be honest, it would be much easier if both equities and commodities could be traded using funds from the same account, but that's not the way it is, at least right now.

The problem is largely regulatory. The Commodity Futures Trading Commission (CFTC), which regulates commodities, and the Securities and Exchange Commission (SEC), which regulates stocks, are separate government entities. The two agencies require that trading funds not be "commingled"—in other words, one account can't be used to clear both stocks and futures. Nowadays many firms trade both equities and commodities, but they still require you to have two separate accounts for this very reason. This may change someday, but it hasn't yet.

Opening an Account

The process may seem daunting at first, but it's really not. Today many firms have online account applications or, if you prefer, they can fax the forms to you. Eventually, though, they'll need a signed, hard copy of the forms. Funding can be done by check or wire transfer. A qualified broker at the firm can help you decide what account is best for you, types of trading (electronic or broker-assisted), and rates. Once you've completed the forms, the broker will submit them to the firm's compliance office; then once you fund the account, you're all set to go. The last time I opened an account it took about four days.

It's much easier if you already have an account at another firm. In that case, you would simply fill out an account transfer form, and all of your current positions and funds would be transferred. It's no harder than opening a checking account.

Self-Directed versus Assisted Accounts

I was a broker for a very long time and I strongly advocate using one, especially in the beginning of your commodities trading career. Sure, it costs more up front, but down the road it could save you a bundle, and even make you one. How?

A broker account, also known as an assisted account, costs a little more because you're putting your trades through an individual rather than entering them online yourself. But it offers countless advantages. This licensed broker will help you make sure your orders are correct, help you place a stop-loss order, advise you of market conditions, and even suggest alternative trades or opportunities. He or she will also keep an eye on your account and let you know if it's nearing a margin call or if you have big gains on an open position.

There's nothing wrong with self-directed or online trading, but it's more suitable for the seasoned trader who doesn't need a lot of help. I personally use both types of access. I use the electronic account to save on commissions for some trades and I use my assisted account when I need to get out of a more illiquid market or need special help. I highly recommend using both types of account; you can have both services on one account and will likely be charged a reduced commission on the electronic and a little higher commission when you use the broker.

This brings me to one of the most important things you'll do in your commodities trading career: choosing a broker.

Finding the Right Broker for You

The very best golfers all have caddies. I strongly suggest that, to improve your trading score, you find a broker who will be your partner for profits.

Choosing a broker is one of the most important, and often one of the most difficult, things a trader must do. I can't stress enough how crucial it is to have a good broker, even for me. Yes, I, in my infinite Maniac Trader wisdom, still need a broker. Why? Simple: for the same reason the saying "He who represents himself has a fool for a lawyer" applies to this scenario. That doesn't mean I'm not able to trade without a broker; what it means is that it's always good to have someone impartial to help you decide the best course of action.

This individual doesn't take things personally—he or she can set aside emotions in a way that you may not be able to. I can't tell you the number of times my broker, Charlie, has talked me in off the ledge when a trade is going against me. He'll remind me why I put the position on in the first place and help me stay focused and not panic.

HOW DO I FIND A BROKER AND WHAT QUESTIONS SHOULD I ASK?

There are thousands of brokers; the Internet is the best place to look. I suggest financial chat rooms, where you can talk to other commodities traders. Word of mouth, in my opinion, is the best advertising.

The key questions to ask a potential broker are pretty simple:

- How much are commissions and what do they include—in other words, what am I getting for my money?
- What is your firm's CFTC history—in other words, has it been in trouble?
- What online platform do you use?
- How much experience do you have? (I suggest someone with at least five years or more.)
- How many clients do you have? If a broker has too many, you may find that you get lost in the shuffle or that you can't get the teaching time you need.

Ask many questions and make sure you feel comfortable with this person; after all, you'll be paying the person a lot of money, and your earning potential will be affected by him or her. Think of it as interviewing someone for a job, because that's what you are doing. You're the boss—if something doesn't feel right, move on.

Charlie also helps me keep an eye on my positions and takes care of any problems with my accounts. In addition, a good broker will suggest better trading strategies and provide you with valuable information he or she gets from the market and trading floor.

You Get What You Pay For—or Do You?

A note on paying full-service commissions: You don't always get what you pay for, and it's important to shop around. Always ask the potential broker exactly what you'll get for that commission fee. Remember, cheaper certainly doesn't always mean better, but make sure that you're getting all that those fees promise.

Due Diligence: Do Your Homework!

You must use due diligence when picking a broker. Research the firm and the broker's personal history. This is simple to do; all firms and brokers are registered with the National Futures Association (NFA), and each is assigned a license number. You can access both firm and broker history on the NFA web site: You will find out how long they've been registered, where, and so on.

Both firms and individuals who've had problems with the CFTC or NFA are listed at the top of the site. But keep in mind that a firm with some cases listed isn't necessarily a bad proposition; most firms, especially the larger ones, will invariably have violations and the like from time to time. This doesn't make them bad. However, an excessive number of cases or claims is a red flag, depending on the size of the firm. Individual brokers who have several CFTC or NFA arbitration claims also should be looked into a little more closely. Simply ask the person what those claims were about, and if you're uncomfortable, move on to the next broker on your list. It's as easy as that.

Remember that your relationship with your broker is something that you should not take lightly. On one hand, it's a business relationship; on the other, it's very personal. I know traders who've had the same broker for years—some of these broker relationships last longer than their marriages! The most important questions to ask are: Do I like this person? Does the person seem easy to work with? Does the person have my best interests at heart? Your answers to these questions are the best guide to picking a broker, hands-down.

Funding an Account: How Much Do I Need?

Here's another frequent question that comes up at dinner parties, lectures, and in my mailbag: How much money do I need to start? The answers to that are as numerous as there are traders. It's impossible to answer such a general question; it really needs a financial advisor or broker to address it. A million dollars, for example, may or may not be a lot of money to me or you based on our respective net worth and investment objectives; it's all relative.

The one thing to keep in mind is that commodities are highly speculative; if anyone tells you different, run, don't walk, away! (*Speculation* is not a bad word, by the way; we just have to respect it.) In any highly speculative investment, it's important that the cash you use is what you can afford to lose without a change in lifestyle. The term for this is *disposable income*. (I hate this term, because who thinks of income as disposable? Not me!) A good rule of thumb is to go over your investment objectives and financial health with a financial advisor or broker to help you determine what's best for *you*—not for your neighbor, your brother-in-law, or that guy on TV.

HOW MUCH MONEY DO I NEED TO TRADE COMMODITIES?

This is one of the most common questions I get asked, and it is absolutely the hardest to answer. I've seen the entire gamut, from $1,500 to $150,000,000. Interestingly enough, I've seen investors with millions start trading commodities with only $10,000.

The fact of the matter is, it isn't *how much, it's how you use it* in conjunction with whatever your trading strategy is. It's best with most things to never put all your eggs (pardon the pun) in one basket. I suggest no more than 5 percent of any portfolio at first should be directed toward commodities. Later, if you believe these markets are in line with your risk tolerance and objectives, then you may adjust that. Remember, slow and steady wins the race.

Quote Services

Quote services are a necessity for every trader. There are a lot of quote services out there, and due diligence is necessary here, too. Pricing varies a lot as well, so it's important to shop around. Go online or ask your broker to make some recommendations about the various services—or even ask what services the broker uses.

Do I Need All the Bells and Whistles?

This is one of those questions that's hard to address because everyone's needs are different. Determining what you need can be difficult. In general, though, there are some major categories to consider.

First, there is the issue of live quotes versus delayed quotes. Delayed quotes, usually 20 minutes to an hour behind the actual trade, are often free of charge. Many exchanges and news services offer these on a limited basis. Live quotes are available for a fee, but again the old saying "You get what you pay for" comes into play. Live quotes are necessary to see the market as it's actually trading. Most active traders, especially those without a broker, must use live quotes if they want to stay in the trading game.

Once you decide whether you want live or delayed quotes, the rest is like buying a car. You've picked the base model; now you need to add the options you want, which can be as simple as power steering and electric windows or as complex as GPS and satellite radio. Quote services offer options that run the gamut from charting capabilities to news services and every other bell and whistle you can imagine; usually the more bells and whistles, the higher the cost. I suggest starting small and adding other features and markets as you feel you need them. Proceeding cautiously helps keep costs down, and your broker may be able to give you a lot of the info for free anyway. That will give you even more capital to put toward investing.

Keeping Costs Low

As in any business, keeping expenses low and maximizing profits is vital to your long-term success as a trader. The Internet has an endless number of web sites that deal with commodities and related interests—weather sites, commodity sites such as INO.com, options sites, charting sites, quotes, exchange sites, newsletters, and research. Google search under whatever commodities topic you want and you're likely to get a myriad of listings, all mostly free. You may have to do a little more work and sift through a lot of junk, but ultimately it could save you a bundle. There are a lot of expensive services available, and the people who use them swear by them. I've found that much of that same information is available online for free. So look before you pay.

"Ask and Ye Shall Receive"

One other thing to ask your full-service broker for is in-house research. Most firms have analysts, or their clearing firm will, and they're more than happy to provide you with analysis and commentary most of the time. All you need to do is ask.

STOCKS AND COMMODITIES: WHAT'S THE DIFFERENCE?

Another question the Maniac Trader frequently hears is "What is the difference between stocks and commodities?" Well . . . just about everything. Seriously, stocks and commodities have few similarities. This is one of the biggest hurdles for an experienced equity trader new to commodities. The lingo can be different, the trading style is different, and so on.

Commissions

The biggest difference for new traders who have been trading securities for decades is the commission structure. Securities traders are used to paying a flat rate based on the number of shares. In commodities, commissions are typically charged per contract. For example, you may buy 1,000 shares of stock for a $14 commission fee, while in commodities you may buy three contracts and pay $150 in fees. Don't be surprised by this; it's standard and due largely to the fact that commodity futures are so highly leveraged—with one contract you're controlling a vast amount of the commodity itself.

Expiration

Stock traders don't hear or use the word *expiration* much, if at all. But in futures trading, it's a real presence. All futures contracts eventually expire. An October sugar contract, for example, expires prior to the delivery date in October. Once the contract expires, the buyer must be prepared to take delivery of the physical product and the seller must deliver it. Unlike in the movies, delivery rarely takes place (less than 1 percent of the time, actually); have no worries about a big truck showing up at your house with 50,000 gallons of orange juice or 2 tons of coffee. Most futures contracts are cash settled long before that would ever happen. It's always important to remember that futures contracts do expire, and traders need to keep an eye on that time decay—no such thing as buying them and forgetting them.

In Short . . .

One other big difference between stocks and commodities: Shorting futures, unlike securities, is as simple as 1–2–3; it's just as easy to play the downside with commodities as it is the upside. Seasoned equity traders often find it hard to grasp the concept of selling a commodity they don't own. That's right—you can short a commodity you don't own as easily as you can buy it, and there are no special requirements as there are with stocks. If you think cattle prices are going up, you can buy futures; if you think they're going down, you can simply sell a futures contract. Options are a different story, though. Buying options has little or no restrictions because there's limited risk (amount of premium you pay). However, selling or shorting options comes with a slew of requirements due to unlimited risk factors at work. Those considering shorting options on futures should consult their broker or financial advisor.

Margins and Margin Policies

The dreaded "M" word can scare a lot of new traders, but it shouldn't. Unlike in the stock market, where margin is a down payment, futures margin is like a performance bond to protect you, the firm, and the integrity of the exchange. When the market moves against you, and your account gets close to margin call level, your broker (or that

WHY TRADE OPTIONS AND NOT JUST FUTURES?

We fear what we don't understand—it's human nature. Options may sound scary; I know I was intimidated the first time I heard people talking about them. Some of the books out there on options read like a nuclear physicist training manual. There are Greek letters, schematics, and theory after theory. It's enough to scare anyone away. The bottom line is that futures are great but they require margin. Nothing wrong with that, except sometimes investors don't want to tie up all those funds, which need to stay in place as long as you hold the trade. For example, one crude oil contract requires around $5,000 margin; that's a lot of equity to tie up for an extended period of time.

Options don't require margin when you buy them. You simply pay a premium (fee to buy) and that's it. Also, futures have theoretically unlimited risk. However, when buying options, you have limited risk. The most you can lose is the premium you paid. Many people prefer options for the limited risk and the fact that there are no (buyside) margin requirements.

margin clerk!) will let you know. It's important to talk openly with your broker about the firm's margin policy so you have a complete understanding and no surprises later. If the broker is reluctant to talk about it, that could be a warning sign of problems that could crop up down the road. Be proactive, ask up front, and be clear and concise about how you intend to handle a margin call if and when you get one (and you will, I guarantee it!).

MARKETS TO AVOID AT ALL COSTS

Every trader, whether experienced or not, should avoid certain markets under certain conditions, such as the following.

The Danger of Thin Markets

Steer clear of thinly traded markets. These markets don't provide enough liquidity for the investor to get in and out of a trade with a

---

IS IT A BAD IDEA TO TRADE IN THE OVERNIGHT MARKETS?

This is a question that can't be answered except on a one-on-one basis. The overnight markets offer many opportunities for the experienced trader. The bottom line is that some of the overnight markets can be very thinly traded, and therefore I feel they should be used to exit positions or enter on a limit order. Never use a market order or stop in the overnight market.

---

good price, if at all. Often these markets move quickly and can chew up and spit out a trader just like that. New commodity contracts are often thinly traded, as are the overnight markets, usually. Check volumes and open interest, and, as with everything else, ask your broker.

Big Margin Contracts: Risk/Reward Value

Risk/reward is always something to weigh carefully. Examine how much risk you're willing to take on a specific trade in a commodity, and then make sure your reward objective is at least that much. If you're not very confident in that specific commodity, then move on to another and come back to it later. Never risk more than you're hoping to make—that's a surefire plan for disaster.

ARE THERE CERTAIN MARKETS YOU WON'T TRADE?

Sure, I won't trade any market I don't understand. I will never rule out trading any market as long as I understand how it works, what my risk is, and how much profit I can make. Markets and commodity contracts are introduced all the time. Some go on to be highly successful, like the e-mini S&P or natural gas; others are destined for failure, like the frozen tiger shrimp contract I mentioned in Chapter 9. Never say "never." The heating oil contract was what saved the New York Mercantile Exchange from bankruptcy; before that, the main commodity on the exchange was potatoes, and that contract was dying out. Heating oil became one of the most widely traded futures contracts in the world, so you just never know.

New, Untested Markets

There's something to be said for being the first human on the moon or the first to climb Mt. Everest, but these things come with a heavy price and a lot of risk, too. My advice? Let others clear the path when a new commodity comes out; let them road-test it. If all goes well, you can learn from their experience and save yourself some time, aggravation, and money.

Many new markets are thinly traded and there's no history, so it's hard to chart the future. Wait until there's some trading history and volume, and then, if the market is doing well, by all means trade it. Leave landing on the moon and mountain climbing to those who thrive on extreme risk.

ASK THE MANIAC TRADER

In this chapter I've addressed some of my most frequently asked questions. Here are a few more:

1. **What is the worst error you've ever seen on the trading floor?**

   I guess it would have to be when I was working on the NYMEX in 1991, during the first Gulf War. I was an arbitrage clerk in the crude oil pit, which was gigantic—hundreds of screaming and overworked traders in one of the most volatile markets in history. One day a trader from a smaller independent company and another trader from a different firm on opposite sides of the pit traded a 100 contract crude trade using hand signals. *Not* smart.

   Unfortunately, the signal got crossed, so both traders were now buying the crude oil. This was the error. Actually, each thought the other sold it to him. Later that day, the crude oil market rallied almost $5 and the clerks who check the trades didn't catch the error for several hours. By that time, it was more than a $150,000 error. The two companies had to split the cost and liquidate the position. This constitutes a bad day as a floor broker. Nowadays computer systems and electronic order entry have in many cases eliminated errors like that; they still happen, but very rarely.

2. **What are some of the reasons brokers don't take stop-loss orders on options?**

   The brokerage industry hates risk. That's what margins are all about. The brokerage firm and its clearinghouse work to eliminate all risk in their business model; that's their goal, anyway. Stop orders on options are tricky because options trade less frequently than futures and there are many different strike prices to watch.

   It's very easy for an option trade to move and the broker not to be aware of it. If it does move and a stop is elected, the broker may not realize it. If that happens then the broker would owe the client a fill. Some brokers who watch only options will take stops in the front months, but not many. Typically, I don't place stops on my options trades, ever. I have a level at which to recoup equity, and I use that as a mental stop.

3. **How do you feel about buying physical commodities and numismatics (coins)?**

   The world of physical commodities is a separate universe. Physical commodities can be very beneficial for the right person. Coins, for example, are the most common. Coins, or numismatics as they're called, are difficult for the novice. First, you must know how to measure the intrinsic value of the coin—in other words, its gold or silver content.

   Then you have to value the coin itself. I personally wouldn't know a plugged nickel from a Spanish doubloon. It's vital to know what you're buying and selling; often that requires an expert. On top of that, any physical commodity needs to be stored. Storing 50,000 pounds of cotton or 36,000 gallons of orange juice isn't easy. It costs a lot of money, too. Other costs you have to make sure you factor in are insurance, interest, and transport. Delving into physical commodities, even on a small scale, requires an advanced level of knowledge.

4. **What are your top five trading rules and/or cardinal sins?**
Rule 1: Understand the market you're trading.
Rule 2: Avoid chasing the market—use limit orders, stops, and so on.
Rule 3: Never trade a position beyond your comfort zone.
Rule 4: Never trade just for the sake of trading—be disciplined.
Rule 5: Most important: *Never* get emotional about your trading.

5. **What is the best advice anyone ever gave you on the trading floor? What is the best advice you give?**
The best advice ever is hard to come up with. I think the best advice came from a legendary trader whose name I won't drop. He advised me to always trade within my limits and never chase the market. He also told me, "Every sunken ship had a chart." He wasn't a big technician. The best advice I give: Be disciplined and leave your emotions at the door as much as possible.

CONCLUSION

The commodity markets are not for the faint of heart. They're intense and complex, and can change at the blink of an eye, leaving major car-

---

ASK QUESTIONS—LOTS OF QUESTIONS!

I've said this before, but it bears repeating. There are no stupid questions. If there were, I would get the lifetime achievement award for asking them. Honestly, I've been doing this for almost two decades and I still ask questions every day, even about stuff I've known for years. Why is that? Senility? No, not yet, anyway. The commodities markets are huge, with hundreds of different variations, contract specs, hours, symbols, margins, and so on, and they're forever changing. It would be next to impossible, and foolhardy, to keep track of everything all the time. Ask for help—even the most seasoned traders do it.

nage in their wake. But they can be rewarding beyond measure if you learn them, respect them, and never forget to use discipline when trading them.

By now, you're either vowing never to set foot on a trading floor or a finger to a keyboard, or else you can't wait to get out there and set the commodity world on fire. If it's the latter, which I hope it is, now is the time for you to put your new knowledge to work and start to rake in those profits. I did it, and so can you. Every journey begins with that first step; set aside any fears and go for it. Trading is meant to be exciting and fun, and at the same time increase your wealth, so enjoy the ride. I guarantee you won't be bored!

CONCLUSION

SEE WHAT YOUR FUTURE HOLDS

It's a closed society. It's risky. It's ruthless and unforgiving. It's organized chaos. It's the world of commodities.

I've often said that the commodity futures markets are the last bastion of pure capitalism on earth—I really believe that. After all, where else can you sell something you don't own (without getting arrested, that is), then buy it back later at a huge profit? Where else can you control a vast amount of a commodity for relatively little cash outlay? Where else can you realize spectacular gains from trading both sides of the market? And where else can you trade markets that are so transparent, so liquid, and so secure?

Step onto a trading floor, or view it from a visitors' gallery. The energy level is amazing; it's utter bedlam. Shoving, shouting, cursing, screaming, scribbling, and wild hand gesticulations are the norm. Every day vast fortunes are made and lost, sometimes in minutes. It's like no other place on earth. Even in our electronic society, the allure of these markets is unmistakable.

I urge you to use the knowledge I've given you and continue to build on it—you're already ahead of the game. But keep in mind that trading or investing in commodities is an ongoing learning process—

a journey, if you will. No two days in these markets are ever the same; change is the norm. That's what makes them so incredible. Let's face it—if you want boring investing, there are always CDs and savings bonds.

The resource markets are the place to be right now. Those who have even a basic understanding of resources and are willing to include them in their portfolio stand to benefit greatly. People may call me the Maniac Trader, but *you* would have to be the crazy one not to want to reap the overwhelming profits that can and will be made in the coming years. Go out there, grab those opportunities, and realize a potential beyond your wildest dreams! That's my wish for you.

Yours for resource profits,
Kevin Kerr, the Maniac Trader

GLOSSARY

Throughout this book, I've defined some of the jargon of commodity trading. This glossary will give you a more comprehensive list of terms that you're bound to come across in your trading and investing. It's by no means the most complete or definitive, but it's relevant to what's discussed in this book. There are excellent glossaries on the Web from the CFTC and some of the individual exchanges. They're a great resource, so be sure to use them when you need them.

Actual:

The physical or cash commodity, as distinguished from a futures contract. *See also* **Cash commodity**; **Spot commodity.**

American option:

An option that can be exercised at any time prior to or on the expiration date. *See also* **European option.**

Approved delivery facility:

Any bank, stockyard, mill, storehouse, plant, elevator, or other depository authorized by an exchange for the delivery of commodities tendered on futures contracts.

Arbitrage:

A strategy involving the simultaneous purchase and sale of the same or equivalent commodity futures contracts or other instruments across two or more markets to benefit from their price discrepancy. *See also* **Spread.**

Associated person (AP):

An individual (other than a clerk) who solicits or accepts orders, discretionary accounts, or participation in a commodity pool, or supervises anyone who does, on behalf of a future commission merchant, an introducing broker, acommodity trading advisor, acommodity pool operator, or anagricultural trade option merchant.

At the market:

An order to buy or sell a futures contract at whatever the price is when the order reaches the trading facility. *See also* **Market order.**

At the money:

When an option's strike price is the same as the current trading price of the underlying commodity, the option is at the money.

Automatic exercise:

A provision in an option contract that allows the option to be exercised automatically on the expiration date if it's in the money by a specified amount, if there are no instructions to the contrary.

Back months:

Futures delivery months other than the spot or front month (also called *deferred months*). *See also* **Front month.**

Back office:

The department in a commodity exchange or any financial institution that processes and deals and handles delivery, settlement, and regulatory procedures.

Backwardation:

A market situation in which futures prices are progressively lower in the distant delivery months. For example, if January gold is quoted at $360 per ounce and June gold is $355 per ounce, the backwardation for five months against January is $5.00 per ounce. (Backwardation is the opposite of *contango.*) *See also* **Inverted market.**

Basis point:

The measurement of a change in the yield of a debt security. One basis point equals $\frac{1}{100}$ of 1 percent.

Basis quote:

Offer or sale of a cash commodity in terms of the difference above or below a futures price (i.e., 10 cents over December corn).

Basis risk:

The risk associated with an unexpected widening or narrowing of basis between the time a hedge position is established and the time that it's lifted.

Bear:

One who expects a decline in prices; the opposite of a bull. A news item is considered bearish if it's expected to result in lower prices.

Bear market:

A market in which prices generally are declining over a period of months or years; opposite of bull market.

Bear market rally:

A temporary rise in prices during a bear market. *See also* **Correction.**

Bear spread:

(1) The simultaneous purchase and sale of two futures contracts in the same or related commodities to profit from a decline in prices, but at the same time limiting the potential loss if prices don't fall. In commodities, the trader would sell a nearby delivery and buy a deferred delivery. (2) A strategy involving the simultaneous purchase and sale of options of the same class and expiration date, but with different strike prices. For example, in a bear call spread, the purchased option has a higher exercise price than the option that is sold. Also called *bear vertical spread*.

Beta (beta coefficient):

A way of measuring the variability of rate of return or value of a stock or portfolio compared to that of the overall market, typically used as a measure of risk.

Bid:

An offer to buy a specific quantity of a commodity at a certain price.

Bid-ask spread:

The difference between the bid price and the ask or offer price.

Blackboard trading:

The practice, no longer used, of buying and selling commodities by posting prices on a blackboard on a wall of a commodity exchange.

Black-Scholes model:

An option pricing model developed by Fischer Black and Myron Scholes for securities options and later refined by Black for options on futures.

Break:

A rapid and sharp price decline.

Broker:

A person paid a fee or commission for executing buy or sell orders for a customer. In commodity futures trading, the term may refer to: (1) floor broker (FB), a person who actually executes orders on the trading floor of an exchange; (2) account executive or associated person (AP), the person who deals with customers in the offices of futures commission merchants; or (3) the futures commission merchant (FCM).

Bull:

One who expects a rise in prices; the opposite of bear. A news item is considered bullish if it's expected to result in higher prices.

Bullion:

Bars or ingots of precious metals, usually cast in standardized sizes.

Bull market:

A market in which prices generally are rising over a period of months or years; opposite of bear market.

Bull spread:

(1) The simultaneous purchase and sale of two futures contracts in the same or related commodities to profit from a rise in prices, but at the same time limiting the potential loss if prices don't rise. In commodities, the trader would buy the nearby delivery and sell the deferred. (2) A strategy involving the simultaneous purchase and sale of options of the same class and expiration date but different strike prices. For example, in a call bull spread, the purchased option has a lower exercise price than the sold option. Also called *bull vertical spread.*

Buoyant:

A market in which prices tend to rise easily with a considerable show of strength.

Butterfly spread:

A three-legged option spread in which each leg has the same expiration date but different strike prices. For example, a butterfly spread in soybean call options might consist of one long call at a $5.50 strike price, two short calls at a $6.00 strike price, and one long call at a $6.50 strike price.

Buyer:

One who takes a long futures position or buys an option. An option buyer is also called a *taker, holder,* or *owner.*

Buyer's market:

A market condition where there's an abundance of goods available; buyers can afford to be selective and may be able to buy at less than the price that previously prevailed. *See also* **Seller's market.**

Buying hedge (long hedge):

The practice of buying futures to protect against possible increases in the cost of commodities. *See also* **Hedging.**

Buy (or sell) on close:

To buy (or sell) at the end of the trading session within the closing price range.

Buy (or sell) on opening:

To buy (or sell) at the beginning of a trading session within the open price range.

Calendar spread:

(1) The purchase of one delivery month of a given futures contract and simultaneous sale of a different delivery month of the same futures contract; (2) the purchase of a put or call option and the simultaneous sale of the same type of option with typically the same strike price but a different expiration date. Also called a *horizontal spread* or *time spread.*

Call:

(1) An option contract that gives the buyer the right, but not the obligation, to buy a commodity or other asset or to enter into a long futures position; (2) a period at the opening and the close of some futures markets in which the price for each futures contract is established by auction;

or (3) the requirement that a financial instrument be returned to the issuer prior to maturity, with principal and accrued interest paid off upon return.

Cash commodity:

The physical or actual commodity as distinguished from the futures contract, sometimes called *spot commodity* or *actual*.

Cash forward sale:

See **Forward contract.**

Cash market:

The market for the cash commodity; this could be: (1) an organized, self-regulated central market (i.e., a commodity exchange); (2) a decentralized over-the-countermarket; or (3) a local organization, such as a grain elevator or meat processor, which provides a market for a small region.

Cash price:

The market price for actual cash or spot commodities to be delivered.

Cash settlement:

A method of settling certain futures or options contracts in which the seller (or short) pays the buyer (or long) the cash value of the commodity traded according to the contract specifications. Also called *financial settlement,* especially in energy commodities.

Charting:

The use of graphs and charts in the technical analysis of futures markets to plot trends of price movements, average movements of price, volume of trading, and open interest.

Chartist:

Technical trader who acts on the signals obtained from graphs of price movements.

Clearing:

The process in which the clearing organization becomes the buyer to each seller of a futures or options contract, and the seller to each buyer, to help ensure market integrity.

Clearinghouse:

See **Clearing organization.**

Clearing member:

A member of a clearing organization. All trades of a nonclearing member must be processed and eventually settled through a clearing member.

Clearing organization:

An entity through which futures and other derivative transactions are cleared and settled. It's also responsible for ensuring the proper conduct of each contract's delivery procedures and the adequate financing of trading. A clearing organization can be a division of a particular exchange, an adjunct or affiliate, or a freestanding entity. Also called a *clearinghouse, multilateral clearing organization,* or *clearing association.*

Close:

The exchange-designated period at the end of the trading session during which all transactions are considered made "at the close." *See also* **Call.**

Closing out:

Liquidating an existing long or short futures or options position with an equal and opposite transaction. Also known as *offset.*

Closing price (or range):

The price (or price range) recorded during trading that takes place in the final period of a trading session's activity that is officially designated as the close.

Commission:

(1) The fee paid to a futures commission merchant for buying and selling futures contracts; or (2) the fee charged by a futures broker for the execution of an order.

Commodity option:

An option on a commodity or a futures contract.

Commodity pool:

An investment trust, syndicate, or similar group whose purpose is to trade commodity futures or options contracts. Usually thought of as an enterprise engaged in the business of investing the collective, or "pooled," funds of multiple participants in trading commodity futures or options, where participants share in profits and losses on a pro rata basis.

Commodity pool operator (CPO):

A person engaged in a business similar to an investment trust or a syndicate, and who solicits or accepts funds, securities, or property for the purpose of trading commodity futures contracts or commodity options. The CPO can either make trading decisions on behalf of the pool or can engage a commodity trading advisorto do it.

Commodity price index:

Index or average, which may be weighted, of selected commodity prices, representative of the markets in general or a specific subset of commodities, such as grains or livestock.

Commodity trading advisor (CTA):

A person who, for a fee, advises others as to the value of commodity futures or options or the trading of commodity futures or options, or issues analyses or reports concerning commodity futures or options.

Confirmation statement:

A statement from a futures commission merchant to a customer when a futures or options position has been initiated; typically shows the price and the number of contracts bought and sold. *See also* **P&S (purchase and sale) statement.**

Congestion:

(1) A market situation in which shorts trying to cover their positions can't find an adequate supply of contracts provided by longs willing to liquidate or by new sellers willing to enter the market, except at sharply higher prices (*see also* **Corner**; **Squeeze**); (2) in technical analysis, a period of time characterized by repetitious and limited price fluctuations.

Contango:

Market situation in which prices in succeeding delivery months are progressively higher than in the nearest delivery month; the opposite of backwardation.

Contract:

An agreement to buy or sell a specified commodity, detailing the amount and grade, and the date when the contract will mature and become deliverable.

Contract grades:

Those grades of a commodity that have been officially approved by an exchange as deliverable in settlement of a futures contract.

Contract month:

See **Delivery month.**

Contract size:

The actual amount of a commodity represented in a contract.

Conversion:

A position created by selling a call option, buying a put option, and buying the underlying instrument (e.g., a futures contract), where the options have the same strike priceand the same expiration. *See also* **Reverse conversion.**

Corner:

(1) Obtaining such relative control of a commodity that its price can be manipulated, by the creator of the corner; (2) in the extreme situation, obtaining contracts requiring the delivery of more commodities than are available for delivery. *See also* **Congestion**; **Squeeze.**

Correction:

A temporary decline in prices during a bull marketthat partially reverses the previous rally. *See also* **Bear market rally.**

Counterparty:

The opposite party in a futures or options transaction or agreement.

Counterparty risk:

The risk associated with the financial stability of the party on the other side of the trade. Futures contracts executed on a designated contract market are guaranteed against default by the clearing organization.

Countertrend trading:

In technical analysis, a trader would take a position contrary to the current market direction in the hope of a change in that direction.

Cover:

(1) Purchasing futures to offset a short position (same as short covering); *see also* **Liquidation**; **Offset**; (2) to have in hand the physical commodity when a short futures sale is made, or to acquire the commodity that might be deliverable on a short sale.

Covered option:

A short call or put option position that's covered by the sale or purchase of the underlying futures contract or other underlying instrument. For example, in options on futures, a covered call is a short call position combined with a long futures position; a covered put is a short put position combined with a short futures position.

Crack spread:

(1) In energy futures, the simultaneous purchase of crude oil futures and the sale of petroleum product futures to establish a refining margin. (2) Calculation showing the theoretical market value of petroleum products that could be obtained from a barrel of crude after the oil is refined or cracked. This doesn't necessarily represent the refining margin because a barrel of crude yields varying amounts of petroleum products.

Crop year:

The time period from one harvest to the next, varying according to the commodity (e.g., July 1 to June 30 for wheat; September 1 to August 31 for soybeans).

Crush spread:

In the soybean futures market, the simultaneous purchase of soybean futures and the sale of soybean meal and soybean oil futures to establish a processing margin. *See also* **Reverse crush spread.**

Daily price limit:

The maximum price advance or decline from the previous day's settlement price permitted during one trading session, as stated by the rules of an exchange.

Day order:

An order that expires automatically at the end of each day's trading session. There may be a day order with time contingency. For example, an "off at a specific time" order is one that remains in force until the specified time during the session is reached. Then, the order is automatically canceled.

Day trader:

A trader, often a person with exchange trading privileges, who takes positions and then offsets them during the same trading session prior to the close of trading.

Deck:

The orders for purchase or sale of futures and options contracts held by a floor broker. Also referred to as an *order book.*

Delivery:

The tender and receipt of the actual commodity, the cash value of the commodity, or a delivery instrument covering the commodity (e.g., warehouse receipts or shipping certificates), used to settle a futures contract. *See also* **Delivery notice**; **Notice of intent to deliver.**

Delivery date:

The date on which the commodity or delivery instrument must be delivered to fulfill the terms of a contract.

Delivery month:

The specified month within which a futures contract matures and can be settled by delivery or the specified month in which the delivery period begins.

Delivery notice:

The written notice given by the seller of his or her intention to make delivery against an open short futures position on a particular date. This notice, delivered through the clearing organization, is separate and distinct from the warehouse receipt or other instrument that will be used to transfer title. Also called *notice of intent to deliver* or *notice of delivery.*

Delta:

The expected change in an option's price, given a one-unit change in the price of the underlying futures contract or physical commodity. For example, an option with a delta of 0.5 would change $.50 when the underlying commodity moves $1.00.

Delta margining or *delta-based margining:*

An option margining system used by some exchanges that equates the changes in option premiumswith the changes in the price of the underlying futures contract to determine risk factors on which to base the margin requirements.

Delta neutral:

Refers to a position involving options that is designed to have an overall delta of zero.

Deposit:

The initial outlay required of a client to open a futures position, returnable upon liquidation of that position. *See also* **Margin.**

Disclosure document:

A statement that must be provided to prospective customers that describes trading strategy, potential risk, commissions, fees, performance, and other relevant information.

Discount:

(1) The amount a price would be reduced to buy a commodity of lesser grade; (2) sometimes used to refer to the price differences between futures of different delivery months, as in "July at a discount to May," indicating that the price for the July futures is lower than that for May.

Discretionary account:

The holder of an account gives written power of attorney to someone else, often a commodity trading advisor, to buy and sell without prior approval of the holder; often called a *managed account* or *controlled account.*

Elliott Wave:

In technical analysis, a charting method based on the belief that all prices act as waves, rising and falling rhythmically. Based on a theory by Ralph Elliott.

Equity:

As used on a trading account statement, refers to the residual dollar value of a futures or option trading account, assuming it was liquidated at current prices.

European option:

An option that may be exercised only on the expiration date. *See also* **American option.**

Exchange:

A central marketplace with established rules and regulations where buyers and sellers meet to trade futures and options contracts or securities.

Exchange for physicals (EFP):

A transaction in which the buyer of a cash commodity transfers to the seller a corresponding amount of long futures contracts, or receives from the seller a corresponding amount of short futures, at a price difference mutually agreed upon. In this way, the opposite hedges in futures of both parties are closed out simultaneously. Also called *exchange of futures for cash, AA (against actuals),* or *ex-pit transactions.*

Exercise:

To elect to buy or sell, taking advantage of the right (but not the obligation) of the owner of an option contract.

Exercise price (strike price):

The price, specified in the option contract, at which the underlying futures contract, security, or commodity will move from seller to buyer.

Expiration date:

The date on which an option contract automatically expires; the last day an option may be exercised.

Extrinsic value:

See **Time value.**

Fast market:

Transactions in the pit take place in such volume and so rapidly that price reporters behind with price quotations insert the word "FAST" and show a range of prices. Also called a *fast tape.*

Fill:

The execution of an order.

Fill or kill order (FOK):

An order that demands immediate execution or cancellation. Typically involving a designation, added to an order, instructing the broker to offer or bid one time only; if the order isn't filled immediately, it's then automatically canceled.

Final settlement price:

The price at which a cash-settled futures contract is settled at maturity, according to exchange specifications.

Financial instruments:

As used by the CFTC, this term generally refers to any futures or options contract that is not based on an agricultural commodity or a natural resource. This includes currencies, equity securities, fixed-income securities, and indexes of various kinds.

Financial settlement:

Cash settlement, especially for energy derivatives.

First notice day:

The first day on which notices of intent to deliver actual commodities against futures market positions can be received. This may vary with each commodity and exchange.

Floor broker:

A person with exchange trading privileges who, in any pit or other place provided by an exchange for the meeting of persons similarly engaged, executes for another person any orders for the purchase or sale of any commodity for future delivery.

Floor trader:

A person with exchange trading privileges who executes his or her own trades by being personally present in the pit for futures trading. *See also* **Local.**

F.O.B. (free on board):

Indicates that all delivery, inspection and elevation, or loading costs involved in putting commodities on board a carrier have been paid.

Forward contract:

A cash transaction common in many industries, including commodity merchandising, in which a commercial buyer and seller agree upon delivery of a specified quality and quantity of goods at a specified future date. Terms may be more personalized than with standardized futures contracts (i.e., delivery time and amount are as determined between seller and buyer). A price may be agreed upon in advance, or there may be agreement that the price will be determined at the time of delivery.

Forward market:

The over-the-counter market for forward contracts.

Forward months:

Futures contracts, currently trading, calling for later or distant delivery. *See also* **Back months.**

Front month:

The spot or nearby delivery month, the nearest traded contract month. *See also* **Back months.**

Fundamental analysis:

Study of basic, underlying factors that affect the supply and demand of a commodity being traded in futures contracts. *See also* **Technical analysis.**

Fungibility:

The characteristic of interchangeability. Futures contracts for the same commodity and delivery month traded on the same exchange are fungible because of their standardized specifications for quality, quantity, delivery date, and delivery locations.

Futures commission merchant (FCM):

An individual, association, partnership, corporation, or trust that solicits or accepts orders for the purchase or sale of any commodity for future delivery on or subject to the rules of any exchange, and that accepts payment from or extends credit to those whose orders are accepted.

Futures contract:

An agreement to purchase or sell a commodity for delivery in the future: (1) at a price that is determined at initiation of the contract, (2) that obligates each party to the contract to fulfill the contract at the specified price, (3) that is used to assume or shift price risk, and (4) that may be satisfied by delivery or offset.

Futures option:

An option on a futures contract.

Futures price:

(1) The price of a commodity for future delivery that is traded on a futures exchange; (2) the price of any futures contract.

Gamma:

A measurement of how fast the delta of an option changes, given a unit change in the underlying futures price; the "delta of the delta."

Gold/silver ratio:

The number of ounces of silver required to buy one ounce of gold at current spot prices.

Good this week (GTW) order:

Order that is valid only for the week in which it is placed.

Good till canceled (GTC) order:

Order that is valid at any time.

Grades:

Various qualities of a commodity.

Grading certificate:

A formal document stating the quality of a commodity as determined by authorized inspectors or graders.

Grain Futures Act:

Federal statute that provided for the regulation of trading in grain futures, effective June 22, 1923; administered by the U.S. Department of Agriculture; amended in 1936 by the Commodity Exchange Act.

Grantor:

The maker, writer, or issuer of an option contract who, in return for the premium paid for the option, stands ready to purchase the underlying commodity (or futures contract) in the case of a put option, or to sell the underlying commodity (or futures contract) in the case of a call option.

Handheld terminal:

A small computer terminal used by floor brokers or floor traders on an exchange to record trade information and transmit that information to the clearing organization.

Head and shoulders:

In technical analysis, a chart formation that resembles a human head and shoulders and is generally considered to be predictive of a price reversal. A head and shoulders top (which is considered predictive of a price decline) consists of a high price, a decline to a support level, a rally to a higher price than the previous high price, a second decline to the support level, and a weaker rally to about the level of the first high price. The reverse (upside-down) formation is called a head and shoulders bottom (which is considered predictive of a price rally).

Hedging:

Taking a position in a futures market opposite to a position held in the cash or spot market to minimize the risk of financial loss from an adverse price change; or a purchase or sale of futures as a temporary substitute for a cash transaction that will occur later. One can hedge either a long cash market position (e.g., one owns the cash commodity) or a short cash market position (e.g., one plans on buying the cash commodity in the future).

Henry Hub:

A natural gas pipeline hub in Louisiana that serves as the delivery point for New York Mercantile Exchange natural gas futures contracts and is often used as a benchmark for wholesale natural gas prices across the United States.

Historical volatility:

A statistical measure of the volatility of a futures contract, security, or other instrument over a specified number of past trading days.

Horizontal spread:

An option spread involving the simultaneous purchase and sale of options of the same class and strike prices but different expiration dates. Also called *time spread* or *calendar spread*.

Implied volatility:

The volatility of a futures contract, security, or other instrument as implied by the prices of an option on that instrument, calculated using an options pricing model.

Initial margin:

Customers' funds put up as security for a guarantee of contract fulfillment at the time a futures market position is established. *See also* **Original margin.**

Instrument:

A tradable asset such as a commodity, security, or derivative, or an index or value that underlies a derivative or could underlie a derivative.

Intercommodity spread:

A spread in which the long and short legs are in two different but generally related commodity markets. Also called an *intermarket spread*.

Interdelivery spread:

A spread involving two different months of the same commodity. Also called an *intracommodity spread*.

Intermarket spread:

See **Intercommodity spread; Spread.**

In the money:

A term used to describe an option contract that has a positive value if exercised. A call with a strike price of $390 on gold trading at $400 is in the money $10. *See also* **Intrinsic value.**

Intracommodity spread:

> See **Interdelivery spread**; **Spread.**

Intrinsic value:

The amount by which the current price for the underlying commodity or futures contract is above the strike price of a call option or below the strike price of a put option for the commodity or futures contract.

Introducing broker (IB):

A person (other than a person registered as an associated person of a futures commission merchant) who solicits or accepts orders to buy or sell any commodity for future delivery on an exchange, who does not accept any money, securities, or property to margin, guarantee, or secure any trades or contracts that result.

Inverted market:

A futures market in which the nearer months are selling at prices higher than the more distant months; a market displaying inverse carrying charges, characteristic of markets with supply shortages. *See also* **Backwardation.**

Invisible supply:

Uncounted stocks of a commodity in the hands of wholesalers, manufacturers, and producers that can't be identified accurately; stocks outside commercial channels but theoretically available to the market. *See also* **Visible supply.**

Large trader:

One who holds or controls a position in any one future or in any one option expiration series of a commodity on any one exchange, equaling or exceeding the exchange or CFTC-specified reporting level.

Last notice day:

The final day on which notices of intent to deliver on futures contracts may be issued.

Last trading day:

Day on which trading stops for the maturing (current) delivery month.

Leverage:

The ability to control large dollar amounts of a commodity or security with a comparatively small amount of capital.

Life of contract:

Period between the beginning of trading in a particular futures contract and the expiration of trading. In some cases, this phrase denotes the period already passed in which trading has already occurred. For example: "The life-of-contract high so far is $2.50."

Limit (up or down):

The maximum price advance or decline from the previous day's settlement price allowed during one trading session, as fixed by the rules of an exchange. In some futures contracts, the limit may be expanded or removed during a trading session a specified period of time after the contract is locked limit. *See also* **Daily price limit.**

Limit move:

See **Locked limit.**

Limit only:

The definite price stated by a customer to a broker restricting the execution of an order to buy for not more than, or to sell for not less than, the stated price.

Limit order:

An order in which the customer specifies a minimum sale price or maximum purchase price, as contrasted with a market order, which implies that the order should be filled as soon as possible at the market price.

Liquidation:

The closing out of a long futures or options position. The term is sometimes used to denote closing out a short position, but this is more often referred to as *covering. See also* **Cover**; **Offset.**

Liquid market:

A market in which selling and buying can be accomplished with minimal effect on price.

Local:

An individual with exchange trading privileges who trades for his or her own account, traditionally on an exchange floor, and whose activities provide market liquidity. *See also* **Floor trader.**

Locked limit:

A price that has advanced or declined the allowable limit during one trading session, as fixed by the rules of an exchange. Also called *limit move.*

Long:

(1) One who has bought a futures contract to establish a market position; (2) a market position that obligates the holder to take delivery; (3) one who owns an inventory of commodities. *See also* **Short.**

Long hedge:

See **Buying hedge.**

Long the basis:

A person or firm that has bought the spot commodity and hedged with a sale of futures is said to be long the basis.

Lot:

A unit of trading.

Maintenance margin:

See **Margin.**

Managed account:

See **Discretionary account.**

Manipulation:

Any planned operation, transaction, or practice that causes or maintains an artificial price. This would include corners and squeezes as well as unusually large purchases or sales of a commodity or security within a short time in order to distort prices, as well as putting out false information to distort prices.

Margin:

The amount of money or collateral deposited by a customer with his or her broker, by a broker with a clearing member, or by a clearing member with a clearing organization. Unlike in stocks, futures margin is not partial payment on a purchase. Also called *performance bond*. (1) *Initial margin* is the amount of margin required by the broker when a futures position is opened; (2) *maintenance margin* is an amount that must be maintained on deposit at all times. If the equity in a customer' account drops to or below the level of maintenance margin because of adverse price movement, the broker must issue a margin call to restore the customer' equity to the initial level. *See also* **Variation margin.** Exchanges specify levels of initial margin and maintenance margin for each futures contract, but futures commission merchants may require their customers to post margin at higher levels than those specified by the exchange.

Margin call:

(1) A request from a brokerage to a customer to bring margin deposits up to initial levels; (2) a request by the clearing organization to a clearing member to make a deposit of original margin, or a daily or intraday variation margin payment because of adverse price movement, based on positions carried by the clearing member.

Market-if-touched (MIT) order:

An order that becomes a market order when a particular price is reached. A sell MIT is placed above the market; a buy MIT is placed below the market.

Market maker:

In the futures industry, this term is sometimes loosely used to refer to a floor trader or local who, in speculating for his or her own account, provides a market for commercial users of the market. Occasionally a futures exchange will give a person exchange trading privileges to take on the obligations of a market maker to enhance liquidity in a newly listed or lightly traded futures contract.

Market on close order:

An order to buy or sell at the end of the trading session at a price within the closing range of prices. *See also* **Stop–close–only order.**

Market on opening order:

An order to buy or sell at the beginning of the trading session at a price within the opening range of prices.

Market order:

An order to buy or sell a futures contract at whatever price is obtainable at the time it's entered in the pit or other trading platform. *See also* **At-the-market order.**

Mark to market:

Calculation of the gain or loss in each contract position resulting from changes in the price of the futures or options contracts at the end of each trading session. These amounts are added or subtracted to each account balance. Part of the daily cash flow system used by U.S. futures exchanges to maintain a minimum level of margin equity for a given futures or options contract position.

Maturity:

Period when a futures contract can be settled by delivery of the actual commodity.

Maximum price fluctuation:

See **Daily price limit**; **Limit (up or down).**

Member rate:

Commission charged for the execution of an order for a person who is a member of, or has trading privileges at, the exchange.

Minimum price fluctuation (minimum tick):

Smallest increment of price movement possible in trading a given contract.

Momentum:

In technical analysis, the relative change in price over a specific time interval. Often equated with speed or velocity and considered in terms of relative strength.

Naked option:

The sale of a call or put option without holding an equal and opposite position in the underlying instrument. Also referred to as an *uncovered option, naked call,* or *naked put.*

National Futures Association (NFA):

A self-regulatory organization whose members include futures commission merchants, commodity pool operators, commodity trading advisors, introducing brokers, commodity exchanges, commercial firms, and banks, that is responsible—under CFTC oversight—for certain aspects of the regulation of FCMs, CPOs, CTAs, IBs, and their associated persons; focuses primarily on the qualifications and proficiency, financial condition, retail sales practices, and business conduct of these futures professionals. NFA also performs arbitration and dispute resolution functions for industry participants.

Nearbys:

The nearest delivery months of a commodity futures market.

Nearby delivery month:

The month of the futures contract closest to maturity; the front month or lead month.

Net position:

The difference between the open long contracts and the open short contracts held by a trader in any one commodity.

Next day:

A spot contract that provides for delivery of a commodity on the next calendar day or the next business day. Also called *day ahead*.

Nonmember traders:

Speculators and hedgers who trade on the exchange through a member or a person with trading privileges but who do not hold exchange memberships or trading privileges.

Notice day:

Any day on which notices of intent to deliver on futures contracts may be issued.

Notice of intent to deliver:

A notice that must be presented by the seller of a futures contract to the clearing organization prior to delivery. The clearing organization then assigns the notice and subsequent delivery instrument to a buyer.

OCO:

See **One-cancels-the-other order.**

Offer:

An indication of willingness to sell at a given price; opposite of bid, the price level of the offer may be referred to as the *ask*.

Offset:

Liquidating a purchase of futures contracts through the sale of an equal number of contracts of the same delivery month, or liquidating a short sale of futures through the purchase of an equal number of contracts of the same delivery month.

Omnibus account:

An account carried by one futures commission merchant, the carrying FCM, for another futures commission merchant, the originating FCM, in which the transactions of two or more persons, who are customers of the originating FCM, are combined and carried by the carrying FCM. Omnibus account titles must clearly show that the funds and trades belong to customers of the originating FCM. An originating broker must use an omnibus account to execute or clear trades for customers at a particular exchange where it does not have trading or clearing privileges.

One-cancels-the-other (OCO) order:

A pair of orders, typically limit orders, whereby if one order is filled, the other order will automatically be canceled. For example, an OCO order might consist of an order to buy 10 calls with a strike price of 50 at a specified price or buy 20 calls with a strike price of 55 (with the same expiration date) at a specified price.

Opening:

The period at the beginning of the trading session officially designated by the exchange during which all transactions are considered made at the opening.

Opening price (or range):

The price (or price range) recorded during the period designated by the exchange as the official opening.

Open interest:

The total number of futures contracts long or short in a delivery month or market that have been entered into and not yet liquidated by an offsetting transaction or fulfilled by delivery. Also called *open contracts* or *open commitments.*

Open order (or orders):

An order that remains in force until it is canceled or until the futures contracts expire. *See also* **Good this week (GTW) order**; **Good till canceled (GTC) order.**

Open outcry:

A method of public auction, common to most U.S. commodity exchanges, whereby trading occurs on a trading floor and traders may bid and offer simultaneously either for their own accounts or for the accounts of customers. Transactions may take place simultaneously at different places in the trading pit. At most exchanges outside the United States, open outcry has been replaced by electronic trading platforms.

Option:

A contract that gives the buyer the right, but not the obligation, to buy or sell a specified quantity of a commodity or other instrument at a specific price within a specified period of time, regardless of the market price of that instrument.

Option buyer:

The person who buys calls, puts, or any combination of calls and puts.

Option pricing model:

A mathematical model used to calculate the theoretical value of an option. Option pricing models typically include the price of the underlying instrument, the option strike price, the time remaining till the expiration date, the volatility of the underlying instrument, and the risk-free interest rate (e.g., the Treasury bill interest rate). Examples of option pricing models include Black-Scholes and Cox-Ross-Rubinstein.

Option writer:

The person who originates an option contract by promising to perform a certain obligation in return for the price or premium of the option. Also known as *option grantor* or *option seller.*

Original margin:

The initial deposit of margin money each clearing member firm is required to make according to clearing organization rules, based on positions carried, determined separately for customer and proprietary positions; similar in concept to the initial margin or security deposit required of customers by exchange rules. *See also* **Initial margin.**

Out of the money:

A term used to describe an option that has no intrinsic value. For example, a call with a strike price of $400 on gold trading at $390 is out of the money $10.

Outright:

An order to buy or sell only one specific type of futures contract; an order that's not a spread order.

Out trade:

A trade that can't be resolved by a clearing organization because the trade data submitted by the two clearing members or two traders involved differs in some respect (e.g., price and/or quantity). In these cases, the two clearing members or traders must reconcile the discrepancy, if possible, and resubmit the trade for clearing. If an agreement can't be reached by the clearing members or traders involved, the dispute would be settled by an appropriate exchange committee.

Overbought:

A technical opinion that the market price has risen too steeply and too fast in relation to underlying fundamental factors; rank-and-file traders who were bullish and long have turned bearish.

Overnight trade:

A trade not liquidated during the same trading session during which it was established.

Oversold:

A technical opinion that the market price has declined too steeply and too fast in relation to underlying fundamental factors; rank-and-file traders who were bearish and short have turned bullish.

Over the counter (OTC):

The trading of commodities, contracts, or other instruments not listed on any exchange. OTC transactions can occur electronically or over the telephone. Also referred to as *off-exchange.*

P&S (purchase and sale) statement:

A statement sent by a futures commission merchant to a customer when any part of a futures position is offset, showing the number of contracts involved, the prices at which the contracts were bought or sold, the gross profit or loss, the commission charges, the net profit or loss on the transactions, and the balance. FCMs also send P&S statements whenever any other event alters the account balance, including when the customer deposits or withdraws margin and when the FCM places excess margin in interest-bearing instruments for the customer's benefit.

Pit:

A specially constructed area on the trading floor of some exchanges where trading in a futures contract or option is conducted. On other exchanges, the term *ring* designates the trading area for a commodity contract.

Pit broker:

See **Floor broker.**

Point-and-figure:

A method of charting that uses prices to form patterns of movement without regard to time.

Pork bellies:

One of the major cuts of the hog carcass that, when cured, becomes bacon.

Position:

An interest in the market, either long or short, in the form of one or more open futures or options contracts.

Position limit:

The maximum number of speculative futures or options contracts one can hold as determined by the CFTC and the exchange on which the contract is traded.

Position trader:

A commodity trader who either buys or sells contracts and holds them for an extended period of time, as opposed to a day trader, who will normally initiate and offset a position within a single trading session.

Premium:

(1) The payment an option buyer makes to the option writer for granting an option contract; (2) the amount a price would be increased to purchase a better-quality commodity; (3) refers to a futures delivery month selling at a higher price than another, as in "July is at a premium over May."

Price discovery:

The process of determining the price level for a commodity based on supply and demand conditions. Price discovery may occur in a futures market or a cash market.

Price movement limit:

See **Limit (up or down).**

Primary market:

(1) For producers, their major purchaser of commodities; (2) for processors, the market that is the major supplier of their commodity needs; (3) in commercial marketing channels, an important center at which spot commodities are concentrated for shipment to terminal markets.

Proprietary account:

An account that a futures commission merchant carries for itself or a closely related person, such as a parent, subsidiary or affiliate company, general partner, director, associated person, or owner of 10 percent or more of the capital stock. The FCM must segregate customer funds from funds related to proprietary accounts.

Public:

In trade parlance, nonprofessional speculators as distinguished from hedgers and professional speculators or traders.

Put:

An option contract that gives the holder the right, but not the obligation, to sell a specified quantity of a particular commodity or other interest at a given price (strike price) prior to or on a future date.

Quotation:

The actual price or the bid or ask price of either cash commodities or futures contracts.

Rally:

An upward price movement.

Range:

The difference between the high and the low price of a commodity, futures, or options contract during a given period.

Reaction:

A downward price movement after a price advance.

Recovery:

An upward price movement after a decline.

Resistance:

In technical analysis, a price area where new selling will emerge to dampen a continued rise. *See also* **Support.**

Resting order:

A limit order to buy at a price below or to sell at a price above the prevailing market that's being held by a floor broker; may be either day orders or open orders.

Retail customer:

A customer who does not qualify as an eligible contract participant under Section 1a(12) of the Commodity Exchange Act. An individual with total assets that do not exceed $10 million, or $5 million if the individual is entering into an agreement, contract, or transaction to manage risk, would be considered a retail customer.

Reversal:

A change of price direction. *See also* **Reverse conversion.**

Reverse Conversion (Reversal):

In options, a position created by buying a call option, selling a put option, and selling the underlying instrument (for example, a futures contract). *See also* **Conversion.**

Reverse crush spread:

The sale of soybean futures and the simultaneous purchase of soybean oil and meal futures. *See also* **Crush spread.**

Ring:

A circular area on the trading floor of an exchange where traders and brokers stand while executing futures trades. Some exchanges use pits rather than rings.

Risk/reward ratio:

The relationship between the probability of loss and that of profit; often used as a basis for trade selection or comparison.

Round turn:

A completed transaction involving both a purchase and a liquidating sale, or a sale followed by a covering purchase.

Runners:

Messengers or clerks who deliver orders received by phone clerks to brokers for execution in the pit.

Scalper:

A speculator on the trading floor of an exchange who buys and sells rapidly, with small profits or losses, holding his or her positions for only a short time during a trading session. Typically, a scalper will stand ready to buy at a fraction below the last transaction price and to sell at a fraction above—for example, to buy at the bid and sell at the offer or ask price, to capture the spread between the two, thus creating market liquidity. *See also* **Day trader; Position trader.**

Seat:

An instrument granting trading privileges on an exchange. A seat may also represent an ownership interest in the exchange.

Securities and Exchange Commission (SEC):

The federal regulatory agency established in 1934 to administer federal securities laws.

Self-regulatory organization (SRO):

Exchanges and registered futures associations that enforce financial and sales practice requirements for their members.

Seller's market:

One in which there's a shortage of goods available and sellers can obtain better conditions of sale or higher prices. *See also* **Buyer's market.**

Selling hedge (short hedge):

Selling futures contracts to protect against possible decreased commodities prices. *See also* **Hedging.**

Settlement:

The act of fulfilling the delivery requirements of the futures contract.

Settlement price:

The daily price at which the clearing organization clears all trades and settles all accounts between clearing members of each contract month. Settlement prices are used to determine both margin calls and invoice prices for deliveries. The term also refers to a price established by the exchange to even up positions that may not be able to be liquidated in regular trading.

Short:

(1) The selling side of an open futures contract; (2) a trader whose net position in the futures market shows an excess of open sales over open purchases. *See also* **Long.**

Short covering:

See **Cover.**

Short hedge:

See **Selling hedge.**

Short selling:

Selling a futures contract or other instrument with the idea of delivering on it or offsetting it at a later date.

Soft:

(1) A description of a price that is gradually weakening; (2) also refers to certain "soft" commodities such as sugar, cocoa, and coffee.

Sold-out market:

When liquidation of a weakly held position has been completed, and offerings become scarce, the market is said to be sold out.

Speculator:

An individual who does not hedge, but who trades with the goal of making profits through successful anticipation of price movements.

Spot:

Market of immediate delivery of and payment for a product.

Spot commodity:

(1) The actual commodity as distinguished from a futures contract; (2) sometimes used to refer to cash commodities available for immediate delivery. *See also* **Actual**; **Cash commodity.**

Spot month:

The futures contract that matures and becomes deliverable during the present month. Also called *current delivery month.*

Spot price:

The price at which a physical commodity for immediate delivery is selling at a given time and place. *See also* **Cash price.**

Spread (straddle):

The purchase of one futures delivery month against the sale of another futures delivery month of the same commodity; the purchase of one delivery month of one commodity against the sale of that same delivery month of a different commodity; or the purchase of one commodity in one market against the sale of the commodity in another market, to take advantage of a profit from a change in price relationships. The term *spread* is also used to refer to the difference between the price of a futures month and the price of another month of the same commodity. A spread can also apply to options. *See also* **Arbitrage.**

Squeeze:

A market situation in which the lack of supplies tends to force shorts to cover their positions by offset at higher prices. *See also* **Congestion;** **Corner.**

Stop-close-only order:

A stop order that can be executed, if possible, only during the closing period of the market. *See also* **Market-on-close order.**

Stop-limit order:

An order that goes into force as soon as there is a trade at the specified price. However, the order can be filled only at the stop-limit price or better.

Stop-loss order:

See **Stop order.**

Stop order:

This order becomes a market order when a particular price level is reached. A sell stop is placed below the market; a buy stop is placed above the market. Sometimes referred to as *stop-loss order.*

Straddle:

An option position involving the purchase of put and call options having the same expiration date and strike price.

Strangle:

An option position consisting of the purchase of put and call options having the same expiration date but different strike prices.

Strike price (exercise price):

The price, specified in the options contract, at which the underlying futures contract, security, or commodity will move from seller to buyer.

Support:

In technical analysis, a price area where new buying is likely to come in and stem any decline. *See also* **Resistance.**

Technical analysis:

An approach to forecasting commodity prices that examines patterns of price change, rates of change, and changes in volume of trading and open interest, without regard to underlying fundamental market factors. *See also* **Fundamental analysis.**

Tender:

To give notice to the clearing organization of the intention to initiate delivery of the physical commodity in satisfaction of a short futures contract.

Tenderable grades:

See **Contract grades.**

Terminal elevator:

An elevator located at a point of greatest accumulation in the movement of agricultural products that stores the commodity or moves it to processors.

Tick:

A minimum price change, up or down. An up-tick means that the last trade was at a higher price than the one preceding it. A down-tick means that the last price was lower than the one preceding it. *See also* **Minimum price fluctuation.**

Time decay:

The tendency of an option to decline in value as the expiration date approaches, especially if the price of the underlying instrument is exhibiting low volatility. *See also* **Time value.**

Time-of-day order:

An order to be executed at a given minute in the session. For example, "Sell 10 March corn at 12:30 PM."

Time spread:

The selling of a nearby option and buying of a more deferred option with the same strike price. Also called *horizontal spread.*

Time value:

That portion of an option's premium that exceeds the intrinsic value. The time value of an option reflects the probability that the option will move into the money. So the longer the time remaining until expiration of the option, the greater its time value. Also called *extrinsic value.*

To-arrive contract:

A transaction providing for subsequent delivery within a stipulated time limit of a specific grade of a commodity.

Trader:

(1) A merchant involved in cash commodities; (2) a professional speculator who trades for his or her own account and who typically holds exchange trading privileges.

Trading floor:

A physical trading facility where traders make bids and offers via open outcry.

Transaction:

The entry or liquidation of a trade.

Transferable option (or contract):

A contract that permits a position in the option market to be offset by a transaction on the opposite side of the market in the same contract.

Treasury bills (T-bills):

Short-term zero coupon U.S. government obligations, generally issued with various maturities of up to one year.

Treasury bonds (T-bonds):

Long-term (more than 10 years) obligations of the U.S. government that pay interest semiannually until they mature, at which time the principal and the final interest payment are paid to the investor.

Treasury notes:

Same as Treasury bonds except that Treasury notes are medium-term (more than 1 year but not more than 10 years).

Trend:

The general price direction, either upward or downward.

Trendline:

In charting, a line drawn across the bottom or top of a price chart indicating the direction or trend of price movement. If up, the trendline is called bullish; if down, it is called bearish.

Unable:

Unless they're designated "GTC" (good till canceled) or "open," all orders not filled by the end of a trading day are deemed "unable" and void.

Uncovered option:

See **Naked option.**

Underlying commodity:

The cash commodity underlying a futures contract. Also, the commodity or futures contract on which a commodity option is based, and which must be accepted or delivered if the option is exercised.

Variable price limit:

A price limit schedule, determined by an exchange, that allows variations above or below the normally allowable price movement for any one trading day.

Variation margin:

Payment made on a daily or intraday basis by a clearing member to the clearing organization based on adverse price movement in positions carried by the clearing member, calculated separately for customer and proprietary positions.

Vega:

Coefficient measuring the sensitivity of an option's value to a change in volatility.

Vertical spread:

Any of several types of option spread involving the simultaneous purchase and sale of options of the same class and expiration date but different strike prices, including bull vertical spreads, bear vertical spreads, back spreads, and front spreads. *See also* **Horizontal spread.**

Visible supply:

Usually refers to supplies of a commodity in licensed warehouses.

Volatility:

A statistical measurement of the rate of price change of a futures contract, security, or other instrument underlying an option. *See also* **Historical volatility**; **Implied volatility.**

Volatility spread:

A delta–neutral option spread designed to speculate on changes in the volatility of the market rather than the direction of the market.

Volatility trading:

Strategies designed to speculate on changes in the volatility of the market rather than the direction of the market.

Volume of trade:

The number of contracts traded during a specified period of time. It may be quoted as the number of contracts traded or as the total of physical units, such as bales, bushels, pounds, or dozens.

Warehouse receipt:

A document certifying possession of a commodity in a licensed warehouse that's recognized for delivery purposes by an exchange.

Weather derivative:

A derivative whose payoff is based on a specified weather event, for example, the average temperature in Chicago in January; can be used to hedge risks related to the demand for heating fuel or electricity.

Writer:

The issuer, grantor, or seller of an options contract.

Yield curve:

A graphic representation of market yield for a fixed-income security plotted against the maturity of the security. The yield curve is positive when long-term rates are higher than short-term rates.

INDEX

FREE: For Readers of the book...

An Exclusive Look Inside Kevin Kerr's Resource Trader's Bible — FREE.

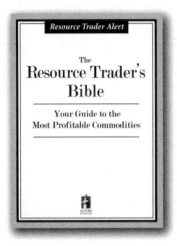

Only elite financial subscribers and members of Kevin's inside circle have viewed this trader's bible. It has helped make his readers an average of **86% per trade in 2006**. Now it can be yours, for FREE.

It's called *The Resource Trader's Bible: Your Guide to the Most Profitable Commodities* — and inside it gives you a lot more than a peek at the incredibly lucrative and "wild" resource market opportunities you might experience around the trading pit.

Best of all, it documents Kevin's amazing streak of **17 winning trades** in a row and his **current 86% average gain in 2006**.

This is **an entirely free offer** — as a way of saying thank you for purchasing this book. No purchase is necessary.

Two easy ways to get this FREE report:

CALL FREE:
1-800-708-1020 and ask them to send you a copy of the report.

GO ONLINE FREE:
Visit **http://www.agorafinancial.com/maniac.html** to pick up your copy.

Upon calling or visiting the website, we'll immediately rush you a PDF of *The Resource Trader's Bible*, delivered straight to your e-mail box.